Racque

Racquetball

JIM HISER, Ph.D.
Associate Executive Director of the
United States Racquetball Association

Series Editor
SCOTT O. ROBERTS, Ph.D.
Department of Health, Physical Education, and Recreation
Texas Tech University
Lubbock, Texas

Boston Burr Ridge, IL Dubuque, IA Madison, WI
New York San Francisco St. Louis
Bangkok Bogotá Caracas Lisbon London Madrid Mexico City
Milan New Delhi Seoul Singapore Sydney Taipei Toronto

WCB/McGraw-Hill

*A Division of The **McGraw-Hill** Companies*

WINNING EDGE SERIES: RACQUETBALL

This book is printed on acid-free paper.

1 2 3 4 5 6 7 8 9 0 DOC/DOC 9 3 2 1 0 9 8

ISBN 0–8151–4463–6

Vice president and editorial director: *Kevin T. Kane*
Publisher: *Edward E. Bartell*
Executive editor: *Vicki Malinee*
Editorial coordinator: *Tricia R. Musel*
Senior marketing manager: *Pamela S. Cooper*
Editing associate: *Joyce Watters*
Production supervisor: *Deborah Donner*
Coordinator of freelance design: *Michelle D. Whitaker*
Senior photo research coordinator: *Lori Hancock*
Senior supplement coordinator: *David A. Welsh*
Compositor: *Shepard Poorman Communications Corp.*
Typeface: *10/12 Palatino*
Printer: *R. R. Donnelley & Sons Company/Crawfordsville, IN*

Cover image: © *Bill Leslie Photography*

Library of Congress Cataloging-in-Publication Data

Hiser, Jim.
   Racquetball / Jim Hiser. — 1st ed.
     p. cm. — (Winning edge series)
   Includes index.
   ISBN 0–8151–4463–6
   1. Racquetball. I. Title. II. Series: Winning edge series
(Boston, Mass.)
GV1003.34.H57   1999
796.343—dc21   98–37352
                                    CIP

www.mhhe.com

PREFACE

In order to become a complete racquetball player, an athlete should understand and practice certain steps. For the beginning player, it is imperative to develop proper technique, initiate proper strategy and court position, and lay the basis for a complete training program. At the intermediate playing level, some refinement of technique is normally required, along with further development of strategies and continuance of a full season training plan. The advanced player should concentrate on the mental preparation and consistency of execution important when pursuing victory. Compliance to a full year's training program stressing proper nutrition, strength, flexibility, mental training, and speed training is necessary for the advanced racquetball athlete to continually perform at a high level.

This book will review the numerous skills, techniques, and strategies necessary for racquetball success. Of course, the definition of success varies depending on an athlete's goals and expectations. For the recreational players success may simply be to keep the ball in play in order to obtain a good physical workout. For the advanced player success may be almost the opposite: to make the rallies as short as possible and to win each point or rally at the earliest possible moment.

▶ Audience

This text is designed for anyone who wants to begin or improve their game of racquetball. Whatever your level of play and your objective of participation, this text will provide information to make your involvement more skilled and enjoyable.

▶ Features

The information provided in this text will allow you to use it continually; basic strokes, serving techniques, and strategies are the fundamentals of any racquetball game. Chapter 1, Racquetball History and Trends, details the evolution of the game, and each proceeding chapter devotes space to the numerous facets of racquetball such as equipment, rules, exercises, the serve, playing the back wall, and much more. One of the many things you will learn in this text is the correct relationship between your body and racquet position. Photographs help to illustrate the movements so they can readily be duplicated.

In addition, some special features offered throughout the text include:
- Professional photographs illustrating proper techniques.
- A bulleted list of objectives for each chapter as well as a closing summary, both of which reinforce the major points of coverage.

- Key words and terms set in bold throughout the text to enable you to build a working vocabulary of concepts and principles necessary for understanding, beginning, and building skills for racquetball.
- Special Fitness Tip boxes that outline concepts, applications, and procedures for quick reference.
- A model (in the appendix) for developing a yearlong training schedule that will keep you fit for the court and for everyday life.

▶ Ancillaries

To facilitate use of this text in the classroom, a printed Test Bank of approximately 150 questions is available to instructors. These questions allow for quick assessment of the student's grasp of basic racquetball rules and principles. Please contact your sales representative for additional information.

▶ Acknowledgments

A special thank you goes to Dalene Werner, who prepared the final manuscript and persisted through the many changes and revisions; to Doug Buchanan and Laura Ranquist, who demonstrated most of the exercises and techniques; to Tim Machan, who spent endless hours analyzing videotape and prepared the vast majority of the chapter on stroke mechanics—his insight and dedication to perfection were greatly appreciated; and to all the athletes and instructors who have participated in and contributed to the knowledge included in this book, especially the Elite Camp attendees over the past 13 years.

CONTENTS

CHAPTER 1

RACQUETBALL
HISTORY AND TRENDS

OBJECTIVES

After reading this chapter, you should be able to do the following:

- Identify the originator of racquetball and trace the course of the sport to the way it is played today.
- Explain the role of each of the various governing bodies of racquetball and identify their domains.
- Discuss current trends and their impact on the sport.

KEY TERMS

While reading this chapter, you will become familiar with the following terms:

- ► American Amateur Racquetball Association (AARA)
- ► Fitness Sport
- ► International Amateur Racquetball Federation (IARF)

Continued on p. 2

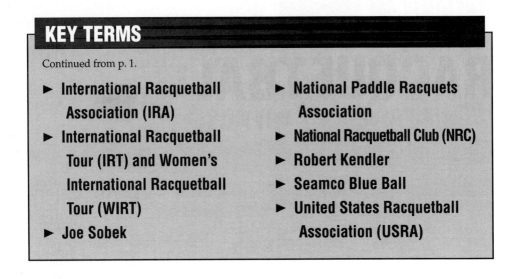

KEY TERMS

Continued from p. 1.

▶ **International Racquetball Association (IRA)**

▶ **International Racquetball Tour (IRT) and Women's International Racquetball Tour (WIRT)**

▶ **Joe Sobek**

▶ **National Paddle Racquets Association**

▶ **National Racquetball Club (NRC)**

▶ **Robert Kendler**

▶ **Seamco Blue Ball**

▶ **United States Racquetball Association (USRA)**

HISTORY

Racquetball is a relatively young sport in comparison to similar activities such as tennis and squash. No other competitive sport has had a faster or more unpredictable growth than racquetball.

ORIGIN

The current game was actually invented in 1949 by a former employee of a Connecticut-based rubber manufacturer, YMCA tennis teaching pro named **Joe Sobek.** An avid handball enthusiast, Joe found the game extremely hard on his hands and decided to build a racquet to hit the ball, rather than using his reddened, calloused hands. Contrary to popular folklore, Joe did not saw the handle off a tennis racquet. Actually, he specifically designed a racquet for his game using criteria he had researched from paddleball, paddle tennis, and platform tennis racquets. Joe's first racquet was made of a thickened wooden frame, with cross strings of nylon. Along with some colleagues from the Seamless Rubber Company, Joe also developed a ball for his new game, the **Seamco blue ball.** The game was ready for the masses.

FIRST ORGANIZATION

In 1952, Joe Sobek founded the **National Paddle Racquets Association** and codified the first official rules of what we now know as the game of racquetball. The game continued to grow, and in 1960 Joe turned the distribution of balls and racquets over to the Bancroft Racket Manufacturing Company.

Although Joe was certainly the founder of racquetball, one other individual was really responsible for the phenomenal growth and popularity of the sport in the

1970s and 1980s. **Robert Kendler,** a Chicago real estate millionaire, became president of the **International Racquetball Association (IRA)** and combined the organizations of his and Joe Sobek's followers. The IRA was a national extension of an association called the United States Handball Association, a group Kendler had headed for 18 years. It was in 1969 that a hard core of players decided to give the new game a new name. Many of the players had progressed from handball to paddleball and then on to "paddle racquets," the new game invented by Sobek that was played with a strung racquet. It was at this time that the name of Sobek's game was changed to racquetball.

In 1973, after disputes with his board of directors, Kendler decided to break away from the parent organization (IRA) and create the **National Racquetball Club (NRC).** In 1973 the first professional racquetball tour began under the NRC.

TODAY'S GOVERNING BODIES

Today the governing body for amateur racquetball (which evolved from the old IRA) is called the **United States Racquetball Association (USRA),** previously the **American Amateur Racquetball Association (AARA).** The governing body for men's professional racquetball is the **International Racquetball Tour (IRT),** and for women's professional racquetball, the **Women's International Racquetball Tour (WIRT).** It has been estimated that in 1995 the number of racquetball players in the United States was approximately 8 million.

▶ **Joe Sobek**
Invented the sport of racquetball in 1949.

▶ **Seamco Blue Ball**
First racquetball developed by Joe Sobek. Today, numerous types of balls are used (produced by several different manufacturers).

▶ **National Paddle Racquets Association (NPRA)**
First amateur organization; founded by Joe Sobek in 1942.

▶ **Robert Kendler**
Major promoter of racquetball and president of several associations.

▶ **International Racquetball Association (IRA)**
Evolved from National Paddle Racquets Association and was headed by Robert Kendler.

▶ **National Racquetball Club (NRC)**
Robert Kendler's breakaway association, founded in 1973.

▶ **United States Racquetball Association (USRA)**
Today's governing body of racquetball that evolved out of the American Amateur Racquetball Association.

▶ **American Amateur Racquetball Association (AARA)**
Governing body for amateur racquetball in United States (renamed United States Racquetball Association in January 1997).

▶ **International Racquetball Tour (IRT) and Women's International Racquetball Tour (WIRT)**
Governing bodies for men's and women's racquetball tours.

History of the Game's Evolution: Important Dates

1949—beginning of paddle racquets
1968—creation of International Racquetball Association
1973—creation of the National Racquetball Club
1984—introduction of first oversized racquet
1985—racquetball officially recognized by International Olympic Committee
1995—racquetball participates in Pan American Games

Since the 1979 founding of the **International Amateur Racquetball Federation (IARF),** renamed IRF (1988), the international body governing racquetball (originally composed of 13 member countries), the sport has expanded to six continents and 91 countries. The most significant dates for international racquetball were the recognition of racquetball by the International Olympic Committee in 1985 and racquetball's inclusion in the Pan American Games in 1995.

TRENDS

The game of racquetball has definitely changed since the days of Joe Sobek and Bob Kendler. The introduction of the faster ball, the oversized racquet, composite racquet structure, and updated training techniques has resulted in a faster, more powerful game. During the late 1960s, the 1970s, and the early 1980s, the game of racquetball concentrated on strategy, the ability to make precise shots, and conditioning. Games were to 21 points, and matches often lasted 1 1/2 hours. Slow balls and small racquets resulted in ball speeds ranging from 80 to 100 mph.

Racquetball changed in the 1980s when a young, brash, muscular St. Louis player named Marty Hogan introduced power to the game. Hogan hit every shot harder than anyone had before. His powerful drive serves and deep court pinch shots were strategies previously absent or seldom used, but other players soon followed suit.

In 1984 a manufacturer named Ektelon introduced the oversized racquet. For the normal, everyday racquetball player this allowed a larger hitting service, permitting longer rallies and, of course, more power. For the advanced and professional player the game changed to power and speed. To alleviate the dominance of power on serves the professional game adapted "the one serve rule." This new rule introduced to the professional in 1992 reduced the dominance of the serve and resulted in more rallies. Since 1984 numerous manufacturers have developed composite-structured racquets, again increasing the power available to players.

Fitness Facts

"One of the best sports for burning calories."
(*Men's Health*, 1989)

"Average player runs 1 1/2 miles during a normal match."
(AARA, 1987)

"A racquetball player works at constant rate of 75–85 % of maximum heart rate."

(AARA, 1989)

Racquetball's fitness qualities also played an important role in its popularity and growth as a recreational sport. The box above lists a few testimonials to the fitness aspect of the sport.

Today's trend combines racquetball as a **fitness sport** and as a competitive recreational activity. Racquetball fits into the modern, busy activity schedule of many of today's population, producing a great calorie-burning workout and a competitive, mentally challenging activity.

SUMMARY

- No sport has had faster or more unprecedented growth than racquetball.
- Joe Sobek invented the sport in 1949.
- Today there are governing bodies for professional, amateur, and international players.
- Racquetball has evolved into game dominated by power and speed.
- Racquetball is a great fitness sport, combining cardiovascular endurance, muscular strength, flexibility, and caloric consumption.

▶ **International Amateur Racquetball Federation (IARF)**
Founded in 1979, this is the international governing body of racquetball, currently called IRF.

▶ **Fitness Sport**
A sport that gives health benefits by providing a great workout (racquetball fulfills the requirement and is also a competitive recreational activity).

CHAPTER 2

ESSENTIAL
EQUIPMENT

OBJECTIVES

After reading this chapter, you should be able to do the following:

* Determine factors important in selecting racquets, strings, grips, shoes, eyeguards, and balls.

KEY TERMS

While reading this chapter, you will become familiar with the following terms:

► Eyeguards
► Gloves
► Grip Size
► Hand-Laid Composition
► Injection-molded
► Quadriform
► Standard, Midsize, Oversized

► String Performance
► Supinated, Neutral, Pronated
► Sweet Spot
► Teardrop

THE RACQUET

The following will assist you in selecting a racquet that fits your budget, style of play, and skill level:

- Cost—dependent on your budget, you can purchase racquets from $15 to $250. Within each price range there is normally a wide selection of racquets from different manufacturers. If you are just beginning to play the game, you may want to rent or borrow a racquet to use until you determine your style of play.
- Style of play—racquets are manufactured to fit every type of game style. Some people are control players, while others are considered power-type players. Some people may only play once or twice a week, while others compete frequently in tournaments.
- Skill Level—as a player advances in skill, in most cases the desire for a more advanced (and usually more costly) racquet arises. A racquet that was sufficient for the player at D level may not be adequate for the player at A level. Quite often a player's game style changes as he or she advances in skill level and knowledge, and thus the need for a different racquet arises.

When selecting a racquet you should consider these six important factors, described in detail over the next several pages: materials and construction, weight, head shape, head size, strings, and grip.

MATERIALS AND CONSTRUCTION

Basically, racquets are constructed utilizing three different techniques.

▶ Hand-Laid composition

Hand-laid composition racquets are hand-layered in complex patterns of graphite, fiberglass, titanium, and ceramic composites. The flexibility and durability of the racquets will depend on the various methods of composition. Fiberglass is used usually to decrease vibration and enhance durability, while graphite creates greater stiffness. Composite racquets are generally more expensive than other types of racquets. Composite racquets can be used to generate greater power.

▶ Injection-molded

Injection-molded racquets are usually more flexible than hand-laid frames. More flexible racquets usually allow for more control, at the sacrifice of power.

▶ **Hand-Laid Composition**
Racquet construction that is hand-layered in complex patterns of graphite, fiberglass, titanium, and ceramic composites. Flexibility and durability differ, depending on the racquet's composition.

▶ **Injection-molded**
Type of racquet frame that is more flexible than hand-laid frames. The greater flexibility allows for more control, at the sacrifice of power.

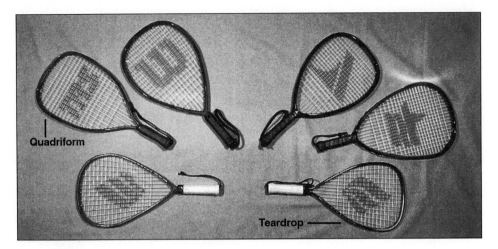

FIGURE 2-1 Various racquet shapes and sizes—the quadriform versus the teardrop shape.

▶ Metal Racquets

Metal racquets are the most durable and, at the same time, generally least expensive racquets. Steel racquets are normally stiffer than aluminum racquets. Which type of metal racquet you select is usually determined by your game style. The more powerful players tend to select steel racquets.

WEIGHT

Racquetball racquets usually range in weight from 195 to 255 grams. Individual preference will determine which weight of racquet is purchased. Heavier racquets are usually preferred by the more advanced and more powerful players.

HEAD SHAPE

A racquet head is shaped either **quadriform** or **teardrop** (Figure 2-1). A quadriform racquet has an elongated sweet spot and is stiff at the tip, while a teardrop racquet has a broader face with more of the sweet spot at the tip. The **sweet spot** is the part of the racquet face which the ball should hit to maximize power and control.

HEAD SIZE

Racquets come in three head sizes: **standard, midsize, and oversized**.

▶ Standard Size

Racquets with standard size heads are usually used by beginning players since such racquets are normally less expensive and are made of durable material. The reduced head size (60 to 65 square inches) allows for greater maneuverability.

▶ Midsize

Midsize racquets are favored by intermediate and advanced players. Head sizes range from 70 to 85 square inches. The larger head size provides a larger sweet spot and increased power.

▶ Oversized

Oversized racquets have a surface area from 88 to 98 square inches. Their length measures up to 22 inches (the maximum legal length). This larger size permits a larger hitting area, which increases the sweet spot to produce more power. This size of racquet is favored by advanced players.

STRINGS

One of the most overlooked areas in racquet evaluation is **string performance.** The thickness of string is measured in terms of gauge. The higher the gauge, the

▶ **Quadriform**
The head shape of a racquet having an elongated sweet spot and stiffness at the tip.

▶ **Teardrop**
The head shape of a racquet having a broader face with more of a sweet spot at the tip.

▶ **Sweet spot**
The part of the racquet where the ball should hit to maximize power and control.

▶ **Standard, Mid-size, and Oversized**
Head sizes for racquets.

▶ **String performance**
The effect of a racquet's string on the way it hits. The thickness of string is measured by gauge. The higher the gauge, the thinner the string, and hence the more power and control.

thinner the string. Most racquets are strung with 16- and 17-gauge string. The thinner the string, the more power and more control. Thus, a 17-gauge string produces more power and more control than a 16-gauge string. The thinner string is more elastic and bites into the ball more.

String patterns also affect power and control. A tighter string pattern (geodesic) allows more control than a wider string pattern (sunburst), which produces more power.

String tension varies from the mid 20s to the mid 40s. The lower the tension, the more power. Many of the power players on the U.S. team and most professional players string their racquets with string tension in the high 20s to mid-30s. When experimenting with string tensions, it is advisable to go up or down in 3-pound increments. This will allow you to evaluate small changes in power and control.

More advanced players are usually able to control even the most powerfully strung racquets. Beginning and intermediate players usually favor the more controllable racquets which exhibit moderate power. String tension is normally indicated in the advertising information that accompanies most racquets or in the more advanced racquets, recommended string tension is written on the racquet itself.

GRIP

A careful determination of the proper **grip size** is critical. A grip that is too small for the user will cause the racquet to turn in upon impact. A grip that is too large may restrict wrist snap. If a racquet has the proper grip size for you, your ring finger should just barely touch the base of your thumb when gripping the racquet. Proper grip placement is illustrated more completely in Chapter 6.

Grip sizes range from 3-5/8 inches (super small) to 3-7/8 inches (extra small) to 4-1/8 inches (small). Most racquets have the grip size embossed on the handle. The smaller size grips permit greater wrist snap and are usually favored by power players. The larger size grips are normally preferred by control players.

Grips are normally made of leather, synthetic materials, or rubber. Although many players have switched to rubber or synthetic grips, leather grips still have their advantages. Synthetic grips are favored because they allow less slippage when wet, while leather grips are usually less expensive. Because there are many factors to consider when purchasing a racquet, a player in the market for a racquet should try numerous racquets before making a final selection. Most racquetball clubs provide loaner racquets of different sizes and expense. It may also be beneficial to consult with a certified instructor who can evaluate your grip size, stroke mechanics, and overall preference so as to provide valuable assistance with your grip selection.

SHOES

Next to your racquet, your shoes are perhaps your most important piece of equipment. Traction, movement, stability, comfort, and speed are all affected by your shoe selections. When purchasing a shoe, you should consider the type of foot you have, as well as shoe design and construction.

TYPE OF FOOT

Most foot problems come from wearing the wrong kind of shoe and not knowing how your foot changes during a match. Knowing your foot type is crucial to buying the proper shoes to help avoid problems such as blisters, calluses, and sprains. There are three basic types of feet: **supinated, neutral,** and **pronated.**

If your feet are *SUPINATED*, it means you put pressure on the outside edges of your feet, thus wearing down the outside soles of your shoes. Identifying marks of this condition are that there are usually calluses on the balls of the feet.

If your feet are *NEUTRAL*, it means you put equal pressure on the sole of your feet, and thus your shoe soles wear equally.

If your feet are *PRONATED*, it means you put pressure on the inner edges of your shoes, thus causing irregular wear on the inside soles. Pronated feet usually have calluses on the inside part of the foot.

It is estimated that two-thirds of racquetball players have either pronated or supinated feet. Players with either of these types of feet should avoid shoes that *don't* flex at the ball of the foot, the exception being if the non-flexing shoes are fitted with proper orthotics by a podiatrist. The best way to determine your foot type and proper shoe requirements is to be examined by a podiatrist.

SHOE DESIGN AND CONSTRUCTION

Shoes are designed in three different fashions—low-cut, mid-cut, and high-top. Racquetball players should wear either mid-cut or high-top shoes because these shoes provide the most stability and side-to-side support. Do not use sport-specific shoes such as running shoes for racquetball. Use shoes designed for racquetball.

Knowing certain aspects of shoe construction such as those listed below and on the following page may help you as you are evaluating shoes for your game:

- Heel collars—These help to protect against Achilles tendon injury, a very common injury among players over 40 years of age.

▶ **Grip size**
A critical factor when players want a comfortable fit, wrist snap, and control.

▶ **Supinated, neutral, pronated**
The three foot types. Supinated means putting pressure on the outside edges of your feet. Neutral means applying equal pressure on the soles of your feet. Pronated means putting pressure on the inner edges of your shoes.

- Heel counters—These stop the heel from slipping inside the shoe and also stabilize the rear of the foot.
- Stabilizing strap—This helps provide added side-to-side support in the front of the foot.
- Cup-sole—This wraps around the mid-sole to enhance side-to-side support.
- Out-sole—This is where the sole meets the floor.
- Mid-sole—This cushions the blow of the playing surface. It is usually either very cushy or very durable.

EYEGUARDS

When you play racquetball you should wear **eyeguards**. Properly worn, protective eyewear can minimize your risk of serious eye injury. The United States Racquetball Association (USRA) requires all players who participate in sanctioned events to wear eyewear designed for racquetball. The association recommends that players select eyewear with polycarbonate lenses with 3 mm thickness. A complete list of approved eyewear for USRA sanctioned events is available in the Appendix.

Eyeguards are of two major types—hinged and wraparound (Figure 2-2). *Hinged eyeguards* are similar to eyeglasses and have hinged side arms. Many of these types of eyewear have adjustable side arms and have elastic-back bands to keep them securely on the head. *Wraparound eyeguards* provide full frontal protection and excellent peripheral vision.

Many racquetball glasses now have special anti-fog treatment and/or scratch-resistant lenses. Lenses and frames should be made of shatter-resistant polycarbonate material.

GLOVES

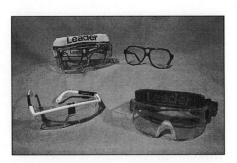

FIGURE 2-2 Types of hinged and wraparound eyeguards.

If you are a serious racquetball player, you will probably want to wear a **glove** to give you a better grip and reduce the chance of racquet turn and slippage. Gloves are made of various leathers and are available in a wide range of prices. Some things to evaluate when selecting a glove:

- Leather thickness—Players differ as to the thickness of glove they prefer. Some players like thinner gloves that permit greater sensitivity and more of the "feel" of the racquet. Thicker gloves often produce greater shock-absorbing qualities and greater durability.

- Inseam construction—Seam position often affects comfortableness and grip sensitivity. Some gloves have cross seams which may affect your comfort when wearing the glove and, dependent upon your grip, could cause blisters.
- Ventilation—Most racquetball gloves have mesh backs for greater ventilation. Since racquetball players perspire so much, it is important that a racquetball glove permit proper ventilation.
- Diving pads—Some players continually dive, thus tearing their gloves. Some gloves provide extra padding to compensate for this increased wear.
- Tab and wristband—The glove must fit snug and not come loose during play. Velcro tabs or fasteners and elastic wristbands help provide a secure fit.
- Glove material—Some of the newer synthetic glove material actually reduces glove stiffness which can occur after several uses.

BALLS

Racquetballs must meet official standards of size and weight to qualify for use in sanctioned events. The standard racquetball for use in sanctioned events is a non-pressurized blue or green ball. Although various colors of balls have been used (yellow, green, black, blue), scientific studies have indicated that the blue ball has the best visibility.

CLOTHING

Racquetball requires loose-fitting and lightweight clothing that will allow maximum movement and minimize water loss through sweating. In order to minimize distractions, official rules also require clothing to be of a color dissimilar to the ball color. Sweatband and wrist bands also help to reduce problems caused by excessive sweating.

▶ **Eyeguards**

Protective eyewear to be worn during racquetball or other sports. Properly worn protective eyegear can minimize serious eye damage. Lenses should be made of shatter-resistant polycarbonate material.

▶ **Gloves**

Worn to provide better grip and reduce the chance of the racquet's turning and slipping. Leather thickness, inseam, proper ventiliation, diving pads, and wristbands are all important elements when selecting a glove.

SUMMARY

TABLE 2-1
Equipment Selection Summary

Equipment	Factors to Consider
Racquets	Composition of frame, weight, head shape and size, cost, style of play, skill level
Strings	Tension to maximize style of play, gauge for power or control, pattern of stringing
Grips	Size for control or power, material
Clothing	Fit and weight (loose-fitting, lightweight clothing is optimal)
Shoes	Type of foot, high enough for ankle support, comfortableness, durability
Eyeguards	Lens material, fog-resistance, hinged or wraparound frames
Gloves	Comfortableness, material (to work with grip)
Balls	Bounce, durability, approved by the AARA

CHAPTER 3

RULES AND BASICS OF THE GAME

OBJECTIVES

After reading this chapter, you should be able to do the following:

- Understand the basic rules of racquetball.
- Recognize court markings and dimensions.
- Compare and contrast alternate types of racquetball games.

KEY TERMS

While reading this chapter, you will become familiar with the following terms:

- ► Avoidable Hinder
- ► Court Hinder
- ► Cutthroat
- ► Dead-Ball Hinder
- ► Defective Serves

- ► Good Serve
- ► Multi-Bounce
- ► Out Serve
- ► Rally
- ► Side-out

BASICS

Once dubbed "high-speed tennis in a box," racquetball is the fastest racquet sport in the world. At the elite level ball speeds can reach 185 to 200 mph. Even at the slower pace of friendly competition, heated rallies and diving retrievals give special meaning to the term "blue streak."

Speed and power aside, in its basic form racquetball shares strategies with other racquet sports. As in tennis, in racquetball a player retrieves each shot in one bounce. Unlike tennis, where points are scored both on serve and service return, in racquetball points are scored only on serve. As in squash, in racquetball the walls are used to strategically place the ball and the player in scoring position. In contrast to squash, however, the lower the shot, the better. Figure 3-1 shows a diagram of the standard racquetball court and its dimensions.

SERVING

Since a player can score only when serving, the serve is one of the most important facets of racquetball. Serves may start from any place within the service zone (see Figure 3-1). Stepping on but not over the front service line is permitted. The ball must be bounced within the service zone and hit before it bounces a second time. If the service hits the floor before hitting the front wall, it is an **out serve**. When the ball is served it must hit the front wall and on the rebound touch the floor behind the short line. After this the serve can touch another wall, including the back wall. If the ball hits the floor a second time before being returned to the front wall, the server is awarded a point. Once the ball is put into play, the court lines are no longer a factor in the playing of points and rallies.

GAME SPECIFICS

DEFECTIVE SERVICE

There are three types of **defective serves**:

1. Dead-ball serve—Examples of dead-ball serves are when the serve hits the server's partner in the service box, when the ball hits a **court hinder** (hits part of court such as the door frame and takes an irregular bounce), or when the ball breaks on the serve. The server may serve again with no penalty.
2. Fault serve—Examples of this type of serve are foot faults (foot goes entirely over service line), short serves, long serves, and three-wall serves. Two consecutive fault serves result in a side-out or hand out, (in doubles when ½ of side is out) (except when only one serve is allowed).
3. Out serve—Examples of this type of serve are double faults, an instance of the server's hitting himself or herself with the serve, non-front-wall serves

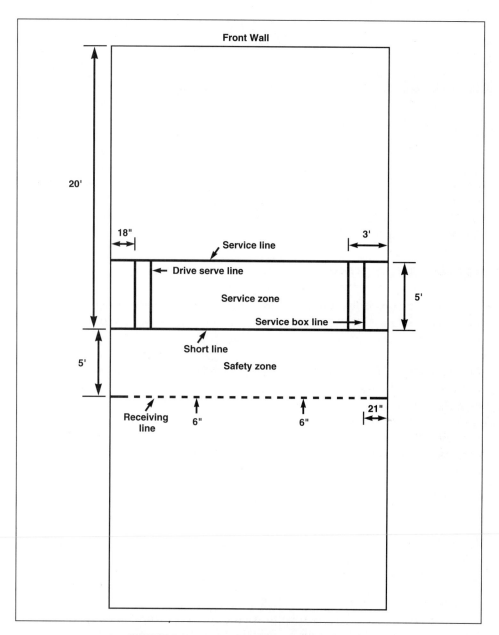

FIGURE 3-1 Racquetball court dimensions.

▶ **Out Serve**
A serve that results in loss of service.

▶ **Defective Serves**
Serves that result in some type of penalty.

▶ **Court Hinder**
When the ball hits a part of the court that has been designated as a hinder (such as a thermostat) or hits a court surface and takes an irregular bounce.

(ball hits side wall or floor first) and, fake or balk serves. Out serves result in an out and loss of service.

RETURN OF SERVE

Once a **good serve** puts the ball into play, the receiver may not enter the marked safety zone until the ball crosses the dashed receiving line or until the ball bounces in the safety zone. The receiving line is the dashed line located five feet behind the short line. If the ball has not bounced, neither the receiver nor the racquet may break the plane of the receiving line when making contact with the ball, but once contact has been made, the follow-through can enter the zone. If the ball has bounced in the safety zone, the receiver may enter the zone and make contact with the ball.

RALLIES AND SCORING

The **rally** begins with the return of a serve. The rally continues until one of the players hits a shot which the other player cannot legally return (that is, until one of the players misses a shot either by skipping the ball or missing the ball completely, or until a hinder is committed). Only the serving player of the team can score. According to USRA rules, the first player to score 15 points in a regular game wins. In a tie-breaker, the first player to score 11 points is the winner.

HINDERS

There are two types of hinders: (1) **dead-ball hinders,** which are replayed without penalty (court hinders, body contact, safety holdup, etc.), and (2) **avoidable hinders**, which result in the loss of rally by the offender.

The rules about hinders are intended to ensure the safety of the players as well as the fair outcome of the match. As anyone who plays racquetball knows, situations occasionally arise when one player cannot get to the ball or cannot take the shot he or she wants because the opponent is in the way. In those cases in which interference occurs but there is nothing that the opponent could have done to avoid it (for example, when the opponent is hit by the ball even though he or she did not appear to be in its direct path), then the fair thing to do is to stop play by calling a dead-ball hinder and start the rally over again.

There are other hinder situations in which an opponent *could* have gotten out of the way but didn't. If another player is taking a shot, an avoidable hinder is something that you did that you didn't have to do, or something that you could have done but didn't, which resulted in a hinder. Remember, while an intentional hinder should always be considered an avoidable hinder, a hinder doesn't have to be intentional to be avoidable and justify the awarding of an avoidable hinder. An avoidable hinder always results in the loss of the rally and a point or **side-out** (loss of serve).

GAME VARIATIONS

MULTI-BOUNCE

Multi-bounce was designed for players 8 years old and younger. It is a great game for instructing young kids. Two lines are placed on the front wall, one at 1 foot above the floor and the other at 3 feet above the floor. If a shot hits on or below the 1-foot line, the player must retrieve the ball on the first bounce. If the ball hits on or below the 3-foot line the player must retrieve the ball before the third bounce. If the ball hits above the 3-foot line the ball can bounce as many times as the retriever wishes as long as it doesn't rebound from the back wall in front of the short line on its way to the front wall.

TWO BOUNCE

In this game, players are permitted two bounces. This means that the retriever must hit the ball before it bounces the third time. This is a good game for athletes who use wheelchairs. Also, for beginners and younger athletes a two-bounce game will permit longer rallies and allow players to work on proper stroke mechanics and footwork.

SCORE ON EVERY RALLY

From 1986 to 1992 the Women's International Racquetball Tour used to permit scoring on every rally, whether the player winning the rally was serving or not. This type of game forces the receiver and server to be aware of every shot whether serving or not. When the game is tied at 14–14, the receiver can win the game with a good return.

▶ **Good Serve**
A serve that puts the ball in play.

▶ **Rally**
All of the play that occurs after the successful return of the serve.

▶ **Dead-Ball Hinder**
Interference that causes the replay of the rally without penalty.

▶ **Avoidable Hinder**
Interference that results in the loss of the rally.

▶ **Side-out**
When a player or team loses the serve.

▶ **Multi-bounce**
A game devised for persons 8 years old or under in which the ball may bounce more than once.

BEST THREE OUT OF FIVE GAMES TO 11

The International Racquetball Tour (both men's and women's tours) play the best three out of five games, to 11 points. This permits players to regroup even if they lose the first two games, and three-out-of-five game matches usually last longer, thus permitting a greater work out.

CUTTHROAT RACQUETBALL—THREE PLAYERS

A good workout which forces the server to concentrate on shot selection and execution is **cutthroat** racquetball. In this game, one player plays against two other players (Figure 3-2). You must serve to win points, and games are to 15 points.

Cutthroat racquetball, by alternating server and receivers after side-outs, gives everyone a chance at playing both forehand and backhand receiving sides. The server plays against both receivers, and either receiver may retrieve the ball (the receivers do not have to alternate).

CUTTHROAT RACQUETBALL—TWO IN, ONE OUT

In this type of cutthroat, only two players compete in each rally; the third player stays out and stands against the back wall (Figure 3-3). Once the server loses the serve, he or she goes to the back wall and the out player goes to the retrieving position. Each player keeps his or her own score, and only the person serving can score.

SUMMARY

- The rally actually begins with the legal return of the serve by the receiver.
- Only the server can score points.
- A rally is won when one player either hits a shot the opponent cannot return or misses a shot by missing the ball or skipping the ball or when a hinder is committed.
- Multi-bounce, two bounce, and cutthroat are some alternative types of racquetball.

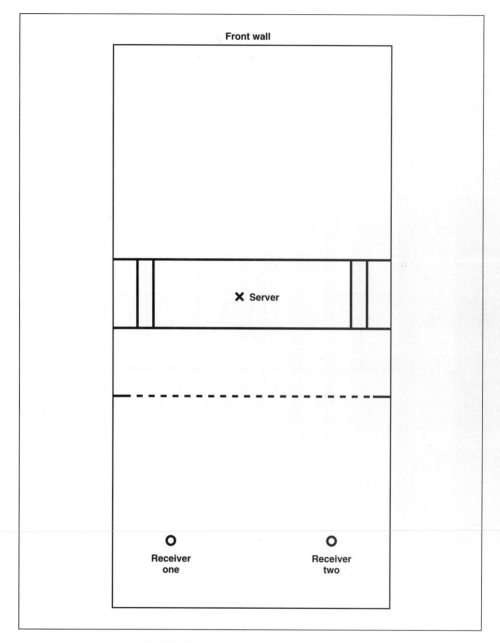

FIGURE 3-2 Cutthroat racquetball—two on one.

▶ **Cutthroat**

A game in which three players compete.

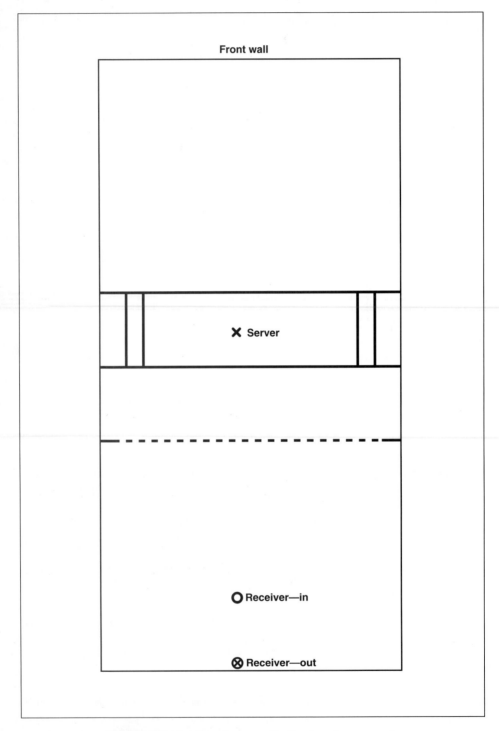

FIGURE 3-3 Cutthroat racquetball—two in, one out.

CHAPTER 4

SAFETY AND ETIQUETTE

OBJECTIVES

After reading this chapter, you should be able to do the following:

- Describe proper safety procedures and court etiquette.
- Outline the basic rules used when playing without a referee.

KEY TERMS

While reading this chapter, you will become familiar with the following terms:

- ▶ Double Bounce
- ▶ Illegal Hit
- ▶ Protective Eyewear
- ▶ Skip Ball
- ▶ Wrist Thong

SAFETY

Racquetball is an excellent sport for fun and fitness, but if precautions are not taken to assure safety, serious injuries can take place.

With reference to equipment, all players should wear protective eyewear designed for racquet sports *every* time they enter the court. Although some players refuse to wear **protective eyewear** for personal or cosmetic reasons, serious eye injuries, which may result in permanent loss of sight, can be dramatically reduced when the proper eyewear is worn.

The U.S. Racquetball Association has a rule which forces all players to wear protective eyewear not only during the game but also during warm-up. Since accidents can occur even when a player is alone on the court, it is recommended that players wear protective eyewear at all times, even during solitary practice.

Players should also make sure their **wrist thongs** are properly attached at all times. When a player has to reach or forcibly swing at the ball, it is possible to lose grip on the racquet. If the wrist thong is properly attached, the racquet will remain attached to the player's wrist, thus avoiding serious injury to the opponent or the player himself or herself.

During competition there are certain safety guidelines a player should follow. At no time should the physical safety of the player be compromised. Players are entitled, and expected, to hold up their swing, without penalty, anytime they believe there might be a risk of physical contact (safety holdup).

The rules of racquetball apply for both competitive and recreational play. When playing without a referee, certain rules of etiquette apply.

RULES FOR PLAYING WITHOUT A REFEREE

CALLING THE SCORE

When there is no referee, it is important for the server to announce both the server's and receiver's score before every first serve.

DURING THE RALLIES

During the rallies it is the hitter's responsibility to make the call. If there is a possibility of a **skip ball, double-bounce,** or **illegal hit,** play should continue until the hitter makes the call against himself or herself. If the hitter does not make the call and goes on to win the rally, and the other player thought that one of the hitter's shots was not good, the other player may appeal to the hitter by pointing out which shot he or she thought was bad and requesting the hitter to reconsider. If the hitter is sure of his or her call, and the opponent is still convinced the hitter is wrong, the rally is replayed. As a matter of etiquette, players are expected to make calls against themselves anytime they are not sure.

SERVICE

The receiver is primarily responsible for calling illegal serves (short, skip, long) and should make the call immediately. Of course, the server can also call fault serves. Screen serves are also usually called by the receiver. If the receiver does not have a clear view of the ball, then a screen may be called. The receiver *cannot* play the ball and call a screen after the rally is finished. All other calls such as receiving line violations and service zone infringements may be called by a player if he or she believes the opponent is at fault. Normally players point out these types of faults and either replay the rally or ask for greater caution in the next rally.

HINDERS

Generally the hinder should work like the screen serve—as an option of the player being hindered. A player cannot play the ball and then call a hinder. A hinder must be called before the player sees if it was a good shot or not.

AVOIDABLE HINDERS

A player who has caused an avoidable hinder and realizes it should call the hinder on himself or herself and declare the opponent to be the winner of the rally. If one player believes an avoidable hinder occurred and the other player disagrees, the rally should be replayed.

When playing without an official or referee it is important to respect the requests of your opponent and make calls on yourself when the situations arise.

▶ **Protective Eyewear**
Eyewear designated for racquet sports.

▶ **Wrist Thong**
The string part of the racquet handle which wraps around the wrist.

▶ **Skip Ball**
A ball that hits the floor before reaching the front wall.

▶ **Double Bounce**
A ball that bounces on the floor twice before the player returns it.

▶ **Illegal Hit**
A ball that hits the handle or is carried (flung) by the hitter.

SUMMARY

- A player should always wear proper eyewear and a wrist thong when on the court.
- When playing with no referee, you should give special consideration to your opponent.
- If disagreements arise concerning a play when playing with no referee, the rally should be replayed.

WARMING UP:
KEY TO A SUCCESSFUL GAME

OBJECTIVES

After reading this chapter, you should be able to do the following:

- Describe the proper techniques for warming up before a match.
- Discuss the differences between prematch dynamic stretching and static postmatch stretch.

KEY TERMS

While reading this chapter, you will become familiar with the following terms:

► Dynamic Stretching   ► Static Stretching

► Flexibility

CAUTION

Before beginning any physical training program, it is important that you assess your physical talents and abilities in order to develop a program that will cultivate your strengths while eliminating your weaknesses.

Racquetball provides numerous conditioning benefits because it is a very strenuous and demanding sport. A complete physical by a physician or a fitness evaluation by a licensed trainer will assist you in understanding your physical status. These assessments are also beneficial in helping you discover whether any restrictions or particular cautions should be incorporated into your training program.

WHAT RACQUETBALL REQUIRES

In racquetball, speed and explosiveness are important qualities you must practice in order to master court movement. Many of the exercises provided in the chapter called "Conditioning for Racquetball" will improve your on-court movement and permit you to get to the ball more quickly. But before doing any speed training exercises or playing full-out games you should develop a good strength base, supplemented with flexibility and agility exercises. Information regarding strength training is also provided in the chapter on conditioning. Although recreational players usually understand and realize the importance of strength training, very often they fail to develop this part of their conditioning program. Thus, especially for this type of player, **flexibility** drills become extremely important pre- and postgame exercises.

Racquetball requires flexibility. Flexibility is the ability to move body parts through their full range of motion (around joints, usually). Strengthening the muscles, tendons, and ligaments allows one to obtain a full range of motion. Remember, in any new exercise program you should begin slowly.

RACQUETBALL-SPECIFIC FLEXIBILITY EXERCISES

Before beginning any stretching exercises you should be sure your body is warm. If you are breaking a sweat, then your body is ready to stretch. There are numerous ways to warm up without exerting tremendous force on your body systems. A gentle aerobic activity to create a sweat (for example bicycling or skipping) should precede your stretching activities. Remember that stretching a "cold" body is like stretching a cold rubber band—if it is stretched too far or too forcibly, something may snap!

Although many athletes still prefer to do traditional stretching exercises for flexibility, coaches of the U.S. Racquetball Team recommend a combination of racquetball-specific stretches and skipping. There are two basic types of stretching—dynamic and static. **Dynamic stretching** requires the athlete to repetitively and constantly move a limb through its full range of motion and in so doing stretch designated muscles, tendons, and ligaments. **Static stretching** may be defined as moving slowly to and then holding a limb position that puts a mild stretch on designated muscles, tendons, and ligaments. We recommend static stretching for postgame exercise and dynamic stretching for pregame preparation.

STATIC STRETCHING

Static stretching should be done slowly, without bouncing. Stretch to where you feel a slight, easy stretch and then hold the position for 5 to 30 seconds. As you hold the stretch, the feeling of tension should diminish.

While stretching you should relax and concentrate on the area being stretched. You should breathe slowly and deeply; don't hold your breath during stretches.

▶ Arms and Shoulders

- In a standing position interlock your fingers above your head with palms facing upward. Push arms up and back (Figure 5-1). For greater stretch, push arms back about 3 inches.
- Stand straight, keep arm behind head, and grasp elbow with opposite hand (Figure 5-2). Pull gently. Keep neck and head straight (do not bend over).
- Stand straight with interlocked fingers behind back. Try to place arms parallel to the floor (Figure 5-3). Fore more stretch, raise arms slightly. Keep neck and shoulders upright.
- Place arm over front of body (parallel to the floor). Place opposite hand on elbow and pull in (Figure 5-4).

▶ Legs and Hips

- *Achilles and calf stretch*—Lean on wall with one leg forward; have your back leg straight with the heel on the ground. Move hips forward until you feel a

---

▶ **Flexibility**
The ability to move body parts through their full range of motion.

▶ **Dynamic Stretching**
Repetitive movement of limb through full range of motion.

▶ **Static Stretching**
Moving slowly to full range and holding.

FIGURE 5-1 Stretch for shoulders.

FIGURE 5-2 Stretch for shoulders and arms.

stretch (Figure 5-5). To increase the stretch on the Achilles tendon bend the back leg, keeping the front foot flat on floor.

- *Quads and knee stretch*—Bend leg behind back and hold with opposite hand gently. Pull leg toward buttocks. (Figure 5-6).
- *Hamstrings*—Sit on floor with one leg bent in front of you and other leg straight (Figure 5-7). Bend once at waist, touching chest to knee. Do not bend neck. Bend over at waist and touch toes (Figure 5-8). For added stretch, cross one leg over top of other (Figure 5-9).
- *Hips and Groin*—Move left leg forward until knee is directly over ankle (Figure 5-10). Move other leg so it is straight behind you. Lower hip down and forward until stretch is felt in front of hip and possibly hamstrings and groin.
- *Back and Neck*—Place left leg straight in front and cross over right leg (Figure 5-11). Place elbow of left arm on inside of right knee and gently push. Turn your trunk as you push.

DYNAMIC FLEXIBILITY DRILLS

For racquetball, we suggest a combination of dynamic and static stretches. The following is a series of warm-up and skipping (dynamic) exercises which will help you move your feet more quickly, control your body movements, and develop into

FIGURE 5-3 Stretch for shoulders and arms.

FIGURE 5-4 Stretch for shoulders.

FIGURE 5-5 Stretch for calves and Achilles tendon.

FIGURE 5-6 Stretch for quads.

FIGURE 5-7 Stretch for hamstrings.

FIGURE 5-8 Stretch for hamstrings.

FIGURE 5-9 Stretch for hamstrings.

FIGURE 5-10 Stretch for hips and groin.

a more agile athlete. These drills can be used as part of your warm-up before a match. They will help prepare your body to move quickly and efficiently, beginning with the very first rally. This will help you get used to the movement, stretch the muscles, and focus on movement mechanics.

Dynamic exercises, implemented prior to competition, are done in a progression known as "continuous warm-up." The exercises begin slowly and gently and go to a faster more forceful dynamic action.

FIGURE 5-11 Stretch for the back.

TABLE 5-1
Dynamic Flexibility Drills

Initial Movement Standing - 5 to 10 on Each Leg	Secondary Movement Skipping 10 to 15 Yards
Straight-ahead skip.	Ankle flip: Skip from the balls of your feet with legs straight. Alternate toe taps with leg straight.
Toe taps: point toe up-down-up-down; switch feet.	
Knee hugs: Lift knee to chest, wrap arms around knee, pull knee to chest.	High knee skips: Lift knee as high as possible.
Karate kick: Knee up, reach out with the heel.	Karate kick skip: Skip with toes pointed up.
Big leg circles: Keep legs straight and bring foot above hip region.	Circle skips: Make big leg circles, foot above hip region.
Foot to buttocks: Bend leg backward until foot touches buttock; alternate legs.	Skip forward touching alternate feet to buttocks.

Table 5-1 shows a variety of exercises that begin with a standing (initial) movement and progress to some form of a skipping (secondary) movement. For example, the first exercise listed is straight-ahead skipping. To begin slowly, you simply stand in position and skip slowly, moving ahead. The dynamic (secondary) movement is to move into a continuous forward skip, skipping from left to right foot, slowly at first and then moving toward a faster more forceful skip.

Warm-up and proper flexibility training is a highly beneficial ritual often neglected in preparation for competition. If you find yourself continually falling behind early in matches it may be due to improper warm-up. If you are bothered by muscle pulls and aching muscles, the above stretches can be done to improve flexibility.

SUMMARY

- Always begin by working up a sweat.
- Muscles should be warmed up before stretching.
- Never bounce during static stretching.
- Dynamic stretching must always be done gently at first, moving to a more forceful action as the muscles become warm and pliable.
- For racquetball, some dynamic stretches should be done prior to the match to "fire up" the muscles for action.
- Static stretches should be done after the match.

CHAPTER 6

LEARNING THE
STROKES

OBJECTIVES

After reading this chapter, you should be able to do the following:

- Describe the basics of backhand and forehand stroke mechanics.
- Use the proper grip for forehand and backhand.
- Outline practice techniques to improve the backhand and forehand stroke.

KEY TERMS

While reading this chapter, you will become familiar with the following terms:

- ► Ball-Relative Positioning
- ► Closed Stance
- ► Dynamic Solo Drill
- ► Effective Zone
- ► Improper Grip

- ► Kill Zone
- ► Rubber Grips
- ► Static Solo Drill
- ► Synthetic Grips
- ► Triceps Thrust

The goal of this chapter is to teach you how to hit a racquetball at the highest possible velocity while maintaining optimal accuracy—and to do it consistently. After providing an in-depth look at racquetball's forehand and backhand mechanics we will use many tools to focus on the interrelationships between court, ball, and body dynamics. To do this, we first provide an introduction to the visualization of preparation and optimal ball contact, followed by a discussion of the importance of maximizing body stability. Next comes a detailed description of the way to grip the racquet for forehand and backhand shots. You will then be shown the forehand and the backhand in great detail; forehand and backhand dynamics are followed by examples of proper positioning for hitting the ball and also for practicing as perfectly as possible.

FOREHAND AND BACKHAND: AN INDEPTH LOOK AT MECHANICS

Hitting a ball with either the forehand or backhand can best be described as a compact motion beginning with the racquet high, then a step toward the ball, then the extension of the arm powered by the triceps to a low flat contact point with the ball, and finally a follow-through that absorbs residual energy in the racquet bringing the racquet back high again. The acceleration to the ball should be extremely quick, but linear, and the deceleration of the follow-through should be the same. Employing smooth yet nearly instantaneous linear acceleration and deceleration yields the highest velocity and shot accuracy.

The simple nature of the racquetball forehand and backhand motion generates incredible racquet head speed and results in extraordinary ball velocity considering the relatively small physical effort that a player puts into the motion. In this regard, racquetball relates closely to golf. A well-driven ball in golf is not "muscled." Instead, a golf pro teaches students how to maximize head speed in order to drive the ball a great distance. The racquetball forehand motion can also be compared to the motion of cracking a whip, during which extraordinary speed is generated from a simple motion. As in the racquetball forehand and backhand, in whip cracking there is an extension outward and a snap of the wrist back inward. The exceptional velocity generated causes the tip of a whip to actually break the sound barrier! If you learn the forehand and backhand correctly, you will find that only a comparatively small physical effort is necessary to achieve high shot velocity.

WARNING!

Because you are about to learn how to generate high racquet velocity, be sure to work hard to follow through correctly. If you don't, you could be placing your body into dynamic overload and the possibility of you injuring yourself will increase.

FIGURE 6-1 Neutral ready position.

FIGURE 6-4 Forehand contact position.

FIGURE 6-2 Forehand ready position.

FIGURE 6-5 Forehand contact position.

FIGURE 6-3 Backhand ready position.

FIGURE 6-6 Backhand.

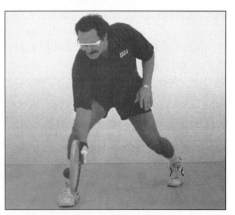

FIGURE 6-7 Backhand.

"SEE" YOURSELF DOING IT RIGHT!

Figures 6-1 through 6-7 provide a simple but detailed visualization showing the neutral ready position, (Figure 6-1) the forehand (Figure 6-2) and backhand (Figure 6-3) ready positions, and the front (Figure 6-4) and side views (Figure 6-5) of the ideal forehand (Figure 6-6) and backhand (Figure 6-7) racquet–ball contact point. Picture yourself doing this!

THE GRIP

One of the most over-looked aspects of a proper stroke is the grip. It is easy to find players using an **improper grip** (Figure 6-9) who still play extremely well. The problem with an improper grip, however, is that you must modify your stroke to compensate for the grip. These modifications may cause numerous problems such as increased chance for injury, greater inconsistency, and possible slippage of the racquet in your hand.

Almost all advanced players change their grips for forehand and backhand shots. Beginning players very often use one grip for both shots, but this approach normally leads to reduced consistency.

The first step in developing a proper forehand grip is to reach your arm out straight in front of you as if you were shaking hands with someone. Place the "V" of your hand (where the thumb and index finger meet) on the top ridge of the handle. The racquet should seem to form a natural extension of your arm and hand (Figure 6-8). The middle and ring fingers of your racquet hand should lightly touch the base of your thumb.

FOREHAND AND BACKHAND GRIP

If you inspect Figures 6-10, 6-11, and 6-12, you will see why it is best to change the way you hold the racquet for the forehand and the backhand. In Figure 6-11, the racquet is being held with the classic grip. Figures 6-10 and 6-12 show that if a player doesn't change their grip for forehand or backhand, body dynamics force the racquet face to tilt upward or downward when the racquet is moved to the forehand. Figure 6-13 shows the grip where the "V" formed by the thumb and index finger is on top of the racquet grip, and Figure 6-14 shows the proper one-eighth rotation for the backhand grip.

If the racquet is flat at contact, fewer of your shots will be miss-hits (hit too high or too low) or will be hit upward rather than being projected on the preferred flat trajectory.

Note: Be sure to hold your racquet firmly, but do not grasp it as if you

▶ **Improper Grip**

A grip which forces you to adjust your swing in order to hit a proper shot.

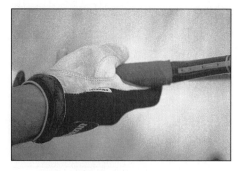

FIGURE 6-8 Proper forehand.

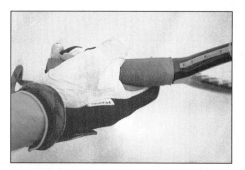

FIGURE 6-9 Improper forehand.

FIGURE 6-10 Racquet rolled back too far.

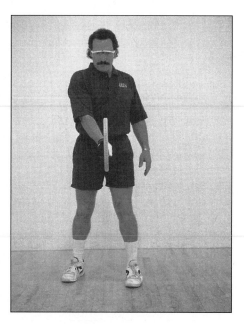

FIGURE 6-11 Proper.

were making a fist. You only need to hold the racquet tightly just before you make contact and while you are making contact with the ball.

MORE TIPS ABOUT GRIP

- The thumb should actually be wrapped around the grip and not extended up the racquet handle. This assures greater control and less turning of the racquet.
- The index finger pictured in Figure 6-13 is slightly extended forward, as though reaching for the trigger on a gun. Some players prefer this stating it

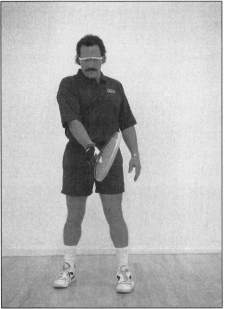

FIGURE 6-13 Proper forehand.

FIGURE 6-12 Racquet rolled too far forward.

FIGURE 6-14 Proper backhand.

provides them more control of the racquet head. Other players use a full grip believing a full grip allows greater wrist snap and more power.

• All four fingers should be kept in contact with the grip.

GLOVE AND RUBBER GRIP VERSUS BARE-HANDED AND SYNTHETIC GRIP

Many players find that the intensity of play causes a great deal of hand perspiration. To limit the slippage this can cause, some players wear a thin leather or synthetic leather racquetball glove. To optimize racquet control and get a better gripping surface, glove wearers usually have their racquets fitted with **rubber grips.**

In the mid 1990s manufacturers began producing extremely absorbent **synthetic grips,** and many players who experience low-to-moderate hand perspiration now use these new synthetic materials instead of glove and rubber. (If you decide to try

▶ **Rubber Grips**
Racquet grips usually used by players who play with gloves.

▶ **Synthetic Grips**
Racquet grips usually preferred by bare-handed players.

the bare-handed method, be sure to wash your hands twice before you begin to play in order to cleanse excess skin oil from your hands.)

Note: If your racquet seems to be slipping in your hand, the usual cause is failure to watch the ball until it leaves your racquet, rather than a bad grip, a bad glove, or an oily hand. (These things can be the cause, but rarely are.)

PRACTICING YOUR GRIP CHANGE

The two most common ways to change your grip are: (1) rotating the racquet using a rolling motion utilizing the thumb and fingers and (2) actually loosening your grip so much that you can "flip" or "throw" the racquet in order to rotate it and then catching it after it rotates the correct amount. You should experiment with both methods away from the court and select the one that is the most natural feeling and works the best for you.

Note: Do not rotate your racquet using your other hand; there is no time for this during actual play.

FOREHAND AND BACKHAND

BASIC APPROACH

On the following pages, forehand and backhand will be covered in detail. Before you look at and read the material, however, a consideration of the basic approach is in order. Whether you want to hit the ball really hard so you can become a champion or you want to play racquetball more for recreation, a few hints will help you enjoy the game more.

Think of the forehand and backhand shot not as a swing, but rather as a snap or slap at the ball. In order to snap your wrist to either side, you want to relax your wrist—and then, as you will see in the pictures in this section, you want to leave the racquet behind as you accelerate your wrist to the ball. As the man in the pictures does, you want to snap your wrist at full arm extension, flicking it through the ball and finishing your motion with a safe follow-through.

Here are two good forehand analogies that help players hit the ball correctly using the proper wrist motion: (1) Mimic the motion one uses to skip a rock on a pond. In this motion the elbow tucks forward, the shoulder drops, and the rock is sent spinning by a flick of the wrist when the arm extends. (2) Imagine shooing away a pesky bug or animal. This motion denotes flicking the wrist with the back of the hand leading (on the forehand, the palm leads). *Keep in mind that when you hit the ball, the racquet face trails your wrist until contact!*

If you practice your forehand and backhand while picturing yourself hitting the ball with the proper wrist snap derived from these analogies, you will generate high ball velocities and an accurate and reliable shot without expending too much energy.

Note: Don't forget to follow through. Because you will be moving the racquet at extraordinary speed, you *must* follow through in order to decelerate the racquet safely.

FOREHAND KILL AND EFFECTIVE ZONES

Perfection would be moving relative to the ball and getting into position so that you would hit every shot in your **kill zone,** shown in Figure 6-15. Unfortunately, few of us are that perfect. Fortunately, if you work hard at positioning yourself so that you are able to correctly step into the ball, you will stabilize your body so that you can make contact with the ball from the leading edge of your **effective zone** (Figure 6-16) through your kill zone and even at the trailing edge of your effective zone (Figure 6-17). On the forehand side, with your shoulder trailing the point of contact (and center of gravity of your body), your forehand effective zone combined with your kill zone is the size of 2 ½ to 3 basketballs! Of course, if the ball is not in the kill zone, your shot will be effective, rather than final.

FIGURE 6-15 Forehand kill zone.

TWO COMMON FOREHAND PRACTICE ERRORS

Figure 6-18 shows two common errors made when practicing forehands: First, this player has failed to move relative to the ball to allow himself to step into the ball to hit it. As a matter of fact, he has moved so close to the ball that, in order to

FIGURE 6-16 Effective zone.

FIGURE 6-17 Effective zone ends.

▶ **Kill Zone**
The optimum place to hit the ball.

▶ **Effective Zone**
The zone which permits a good shot but usually not a perfect shot.

FIGURE 6-18 Two common practice errors. Ball too close to body and forced to hit the ball mid-body.

extend his arm at contact, he will be forced to hit the ball standing almost erect. Second, many advanced players visualize and practice ball contact mid-body, so although the player pictured may have been told to move so he could hit the ball in his kill zone, as he challenged better players, more often than not during play he would be forced to hit the ball mid-body or deep in his stance due to the increased velocity of the ball or the higher speed of play. Unfortunately, players like this one then begin to practice by repetition, and literally program their bodies to move to intercept the ball at the incorrect place most times too deep in their stance. Thus an error occurs not just because the ball is not in the kill zone, but because as the person continues to play better and better players, actual contact will be forced deeper into, and in time past, the person's effective zone! This will result in an ineffective shot and can lead to an extremely sore arm or shoulder and potentially damage the person's rotator cuff. For these reasons be sure to practice moving ball-relative (described in the next section) and train yourself to contact the ball in your kill zone.

THE FOREHAND, STEP BY STEP

1. (a) You should move into position quickly so that you can optimize your shot. This is referred to as good **ball-relative positioning.**
   (b) An accurate forehand begins navel to side wall with your hips parallel (Figure 6-19) to where you want to hit your shot. This is called hitting from a **closed stance.**
   (c) Your racquet should be up and ready. (Figure 6-19). *Note:* Your upper arm should be parallel to the floor.
   (d) Your shoulder should be rotated approximately 45 degrees toward the back wall. In Figure 6-20 we can clearly see most of the player's back.
   (e) Be sure to have your eyes and attention focused on the ball. Make sure that you watch it until you hit it!
   (f) If you begin your forehand as shown in Figure 6-20, not only will you maintain your balance before, during, and after hitting the ball but you will also optimize the accuracy of your shots and maximize the velocity as well.
2. The step into the ball as seen in Figure 6-21 is a step that is a three-quarter stride toward both the front wall and the side wall (approximately 45 degrees). This establishes a solid platform for your forehand. This step also starts the upper body forward and in toward the ball.
3. Once the leading foot is firmly placed on the floor, the elbow is "tucked outward" toward the ball to initiate a powerful triceps thrust (you can readily

FIGURE 6-19 Forehand.

FIGURE 6-20

see this in both Figure 6-22 and Figure 6-23). Note that as body weight transfers onto the leading foot the small amount of weight remaining on the trailing foot is transferred to its toe as the heel lifts. This allows for free hip rotation, which adds to racquet head speed.

4. In Figure 6-24, taken just a fraction of a second after impact, you can see full arm extension, an expression of the end of the triceps' influence on the forehand. It also becomes evident that the velocity one can impart on the ball is also the culmination of not only body weight transferring downward and into it but also the approximately 135 degrees of rotation which adds to the ball the **triceps thrust** velocity.

5. The ball is gone, but your swing is far from complete. Figures 6-25 and 6-26 illustrate the manner in which to complete the forehand. The importance of how you complete your motion cannot be stressed enough. Consider the following: no matter how set you are on hitting the ball as fast as you possibly can, your body will protect itself from your desire if you try to stop your follow-through. There is an amazing amount of kinetic energy (energy in motion) remaining after the ball leaves your racquet. An incorrect follow-through presents an ever-present danger to your body, even though you can partially override your body's desire to dissipate this energy safely. If this energy is not absorbed correctly, you will probably end up at first with a sore arm or shoulder and then possibly, in the long run, with an extremely dangerous injury such as tendinitis, a muscle strain, pull, or tear, or even a severe rotator-cuff problem.

▶ **Ball-Relative Positioning**
Positioning your body in order to optimize your shot.

▶ **Closed Stance**
Beginning position when your hips are parallel to the side wall where you want to hit the shot.

▶ **Triceps Thrust**
The extension of your arm which permits optimum force for your shot.

FIGURE 6-21

FIGURE 6-22

FIGURE 6-23

FIGURE 6-24

FIGURE 6-25

FIGURE 6-26

Study Figures 6-25 and 6-26 so you will not fall victim to injuries of this nature. Note that because your body is going to be well aware of your intent to stop the follow-through, it may actually slow down your swing *prior to ball contact* in order to try to protect you. Be aware of this and attempt to complete your follow-through on every swing without altering your form. Work hard practicing the most perfect forehand you can, and you'll be rewarded with velocity, accuracy, and reliability.

BACKHAND KILL AND EFFECTIVE ZONES

As stated previously, perfection would be moving relative to the ball and getting into position so that you would hit every shot in your kill zone (Figures 6-27, 6-28).

Few of us can actually do that every time, but if you work hard at positioning yourself so that you are able to correctly step into the ball, you will stabilize your body so that you can make contact with the ball from the leading edge of your effective zone, through your kill zone, and even at the trailing edge of your effective zone. On the backhand side, with your shoulder leading the point of contact (and the center of gravity of your body almost directly over the instep of your leading foot) (Figures 6-29, 6-30) your backhand effective zones combined with your kill zone is only the size of two or three grapefruits! Of course, if the ball is not in the kill zone, your shot will be effective rather than final. *Note:* The size of

FIGURE 6-27 Backhand kill zone.

your backhand kill zone is most affected by the interrelationship of the physiology of the arm and rotator-cuff of the shoulder during the swing. The size of the backhand kill zone is reduced compared to that of the forehand kill zone primarily because the position of the shoulder leading until just before the point of contact (Figure 6-27). During the follow-through, the elbow and shoulder are both subject to potential injury. A

FIGURE 6-28 Kill zone.

FIGURE 6-30

FIGURE 6-29 Effective zone begins.

FIGURE 6-31 Common practice errors. Ball too close to body.

proper follow-through protects the arm and shoulder from the energy remaining in the racquet and the dynamic movement of the arm and body after contact.

BACKHAND AND FOREHAND COMPARED

Because the backhand kill zone is much smaller that the forehand kill zone, perfecting your backhand requires that you practice more precise footwork. Most of the sports you may have played in your youth and even adult life are forehand-oriented. Thus, when practicing your backhand, be sure to pay careful attention to drills the instructors give which emphasize footwork. To accept the challenge to make your backhand a powerful and dependable weapon, increase both the frequency and focus of your backhand-related footwork drills. These drills should include footwork practice both with and without a ball.

THE BACKHAND, STEP BY STEP

To hit a proper backhand you will "address" three walls from initialization to follow-through.

1. (a) You should move quickly into position so that you can optimize your shot. This is referred to as good ball-relative positioning.
   (b) An accurate backhand begins with your hips parallel to where you want to hit your shot. This is called hitting from a closed stance (Figure 6-32).
   (c) Your racquet should be up and ready. *Note:* When you rotate to hit your shot, your upper arm will be parallel to the floor (Figure 6-32).
   (d) Your shoulders will actually rotate a full 180 degrees when you hit a proper backhand coming off the back wall. If the ball is coming from the front wall, most players are able to rotate only about the same amount as on the forehand side, about 135 degrees.
2. (a) The player begins both stepping inward to the ball and rotating toward the back wall (Figure 6-33).
   (b) With a proper step and good rotation, extraordinary shot velocity can be attained while maintaining accuracy and reliability.
3. (a) In Figure 6-33 you can see that the upper arm is now parallel to the floor and the player has completed his initial rotation and is addressing (chest facing) the back wall.
   (b) Notice the intense stare at the ball and the almost awkward turn of the neck in order to see it. This difficulty tracking the ball all the way until racquet contact occurs is what causes most players to only be able to rotate halfway to the back wall when hitting a ball coming from the front wall. On the other hand, if the ball is coming off the back wall, turning to watch it makes the rotation to address the back wall quite a natural move.
   (c) Note that the player shown in Figure 6-34 has also firmly planted his leading foot on the floor and has lifted the heel of his trailing foot, which will allow him free hip rotation through his shot.

FIGURE 6-33

FIGURE 6-32   **FIGURE 6-34**

4. (a) As you rotate into the ball, your tricep extends your arm toward the ball. Because the elbow already is pointing toward it, there is "tuck" as there is for the forehand.

   (b) Your wrist should be released so that as the arm descends, the racquet face trails, so that at contact, it will be perpendicular to the floor assuring a level shot to the front wall (Figure 6-35).

   (c) In Figure 6-35 the ball is in the backhand kill zone, just on the edge of the leading foot. If the ball is there, you will make contact with it just as your racquet passes your shoulder. To make contact further back causes shot inaccuracy.

5. (a) At contact the racquet is flat, and you are now addressing the side wall, half way to the completion of your backhand.

   (b) Note that the player in Figure 6-36 is still watching the ball intensely. The only reason that your eyes should come up is that the follow-through will pull them up as you address the front wall.

   (c) The trailing foot is still in contact with the floor, and about 85 percent of your weight will have transferred to your leading foot.

6. (a) The follow-through completes the backhand (Figure 6-37).

   (b) Your eyes will be pulled up to look in the direction of your shot as your shoulders address the front wall.

FIGURE 6-35

FIGURE 6-36

(c) Although up on your trailing toe, be sure not to lift your body and head up until the ball is gone and the energy remaining in your racquet is dissipated by your follow-through. Note that the swing starts with the forearm parallel to the floor and ends that way as well.

FIGURE 6-37

PRACTICING YOUR FOREHAND AND BACKHAND

Because many players practice imperfectly, repeating incorrect forehand and backhand dynamics, they impede their own desire to improve.

There are two basic ways to practice—the static solo drill and the dynamic solo drill—and both are extremely important if you want to advance your game as quickly as possible while still building an extremely reliable foundation for it.

STATIC SOLO DRILL

The first way to practice is using **static solo drills.** For such a drill you go into a court alone and hit one shot, retrieve the ball, and repeat the same shot a number of times. This may sound boring, but what are the chances that you can move into position to hit a ball and execute a good forehand or backhand *if you don't know where that position is and if you don't have a reliable shot, even if you manage to get there?* Therefore, the static solo drill is *very* important. If you are an extremely advanced player with extraordinarily fine mechanics, you will still need to hit static solo

FIGURE 6-38 Static drill—forehand drop.

FIGURE 6-39 Static drill—backhand drop.

shots, especially to warm up your forehand and backhand before play. Be sure to practice hitting the down-the-line shot first, then add cross-court pass practice and side-wall–front-wall combination shots as well. You should practice these from either side and hit them from out of the corners of the court. Set a comfortable distance from both the side wall and the back wall. Your ball drop should be about 1 foot away from the side wall.

Because you may want to emulate how advanced and professional players warm up, keep in mind that the very best players already know exactly how far from their body, and in what position relative to the ball, they need to stand in order to hit their warm-up shots. Thus, it is quite common to see very advanced players practice by tossing a ball into a corner, against the back wall or onto a side wall. Now, if you already knew, as they do, exactly how to address the ball and exactly when to hit it, so that you wouldn't allow the ball to be too close or too far away, copying their toss would be perfectly OK; however, it's best to do other types of practice in the beginning, putting first things first.

Figures 6-38 and 6-39 show a proper ball drop for a static solo drill. Look at these figures very carefully and study them. As simple as it may look, dropping the ball correctly is one of the most important things you will learn about in this entire section. The ideal forehand and backhand shots shown previously in this chapter could not be hit as perfectly if the ball were not in the correct place at precisely the right time.

Please notice that the ball is dropped so that it is falling vertically. The next step is to step back away from the ball (back even with your trailing foot) so that you can look at and learn this distance—the distance which allows a proper forehand and backhand stroke, as previously pictured in this chapter. You need to train your body to stay at that distance, in that *ball-relative position*, in order to hit the ball well.

The player shown in Figure 6-38 has stepped and leaned outward in order to drop the ball so that he can hit it with his arm extended. You have to learn to add a little extra stretch as he is seen doing. If you were stepping out using your normal stride and did not add this little extra distance, then

▶ **Static Solo Drill**
Drill performed by one person in which the person simply drops and hits the ball.

WARNING:

Doing the dynamic solo drill is extremely physically taxing. Be sure to monitor your heart and respiration rate so that you do not strain your body. Furthermore, at the first signs of physical discomfort discontinue the drill, exit the court, and take a break. After a few minutes, during which you can assess the source and severity of the discomfort, you can decide if you need a doctor's or a certified physical therapist's advice. If this is not needed, return to the court and restart the drill. If discomfort reoccurs, discontinue the drill and be sure to seek proper medical advice. If the discomfort is caused by incorrect dynamics, seek out a certified professional racquetball instructor for his or her advice. Often minor strain can stem from a misinterpretation of visual aids or the instruction received which guides what a player is actually doing during the drill. A professional will be able to analyze your drilling and advise you as to how to proceed so that discomfort does not reoccur.

---

you would still be too close to the ball. You would be forcing yourself to make contact with the ball with your arm extended. Therefore, be sure to step back after your drop and wait at least three bounces before hitting the ball in order to learn the correct distance between the ball and your body that will allow you to hit your forehand or backhand in the proper way as shown previously in this chapter.

When you do static solo drills, you should not only emphasize ball-relative positioning but you should also learn to hit the ball only as hard and as low as you can while maintaining control over your shot. The more reliable your shot, the better a player you will become. If you use static solo drills to warm up and to practice, your shots will be increasing in velocity and you will hit them on a flatter, lower trajectory as time passes.

DYNAMIC SOLO DRILL

The second form of drilling is called the **dynamic solo drill.** For this type of drill you will still be alone on the court, but just as in real play rather than hitting the ball then retrieving it you will be moving and hitting it repeatedly.

The simplest dynamic solo drill you can do is to hit a ball starting with a static solo drop and hit, and then keep the ball moving by playing every ball after multiple bounces. Be sure to move in such a manner that you are focused on ball-relative movement. The most common dynamic solo drill error is hitting shots when the ball is not in the proper position, which usually happens when you rush your shot. It cannot be stressed enough that during the dynamic solo drill you must move quickly into position to play the ball correctly and then move with the ball in order to effect the very best shot you can time after time. The number of bounces does not matter—hitting good shots does!

Hint: If you want to see rapid improvement in your forehand or backhand, whichever of the two you consider the weaker (or simply in need of work), try to start your drill with the appropriate static solo ball drop and then force yourself to hit only the "weaker" shot that you wish to improve. Now, you may find this means moving onto the backhand side of your court to play a forehand, or vice versa, but this is a drill so work very hard on moving into the best ball-relative position you can shot after shot.

Remember: The dynamic solo drill is very physically demanding, so be sure to take frequent breaks for stabilization of heart and respiration rates, as well as breaks for water and relaxation.

OTHER PRACTICE

Don't forget to play games. Play comes in many forms, all of which will contribute to your game improvement. Static and dynamic solo drills give you a foundation, but you also need to play actual games! Be sure to play low-pressure games against friendly competitors rather than against those who place you under intense pressure. This will allow you the freedom to focus on a single technique or skill while you play. Playing people with a skill level that is even with yours allows the two of you to help each other improve, whereas playing competitive players may challenge you to work too hard in order to try to play at their level.

A BIG PSYCHOLOGICAL ADVANTAGE

When you do drills for (or play) racquetball, an important key to optimizing your performance is to take the "tense" out of "intense"—that is, to maintain focus on your goals, while staying relaxed physically. In this manner you allow your body the freedom to make all the necessary adjustments in order to maintain ball-relative positioning and to effect the best forehand or backhand shots. If you are intense and allow your body to tense, you sacrifice flexibility. To lose flexibility not only reduces body rotation, therefore reducing shot velocity, but also can reduce reflex time and have a detrimental effect on your ability to stretch and reach for your defensive shots. Staying relaxed does not mean you are so relaxed that your body can't react; rather, it means not allowing the intensity of your focus to affect your performance.

▶ **Dynamic Solo Drill**
Drill performed by one person in which the person has to move and hit the ball rebounding off the wall.

SUMMARY

- The three important directives that will help produce a good forehand and backhand are: (1) move your feet, (2) get in good position, and (3) watch until the ball is all the way to your racquet (and get your racquet up and ready early).
- To perfect your backhand and forehand, establish and stick to a regime of drills that will optimize your performance.
- The more perfectly you practice, the more perfectly you will play.

Acknowledgement - The author would like to make special acknowledgement to Tim Machan and Jim Winterton who provided much of the information regarding stroke mechanics discussed in this chapter.

CHAPTER 7

PRACTICING THE SERVE

OBJECTIVES

After reading this chapter, you should be able to do the following:

- Illustrate the basic types of serves.
- Describe the proper strategies for using each serve.

KEY TERMS

While reading this chapter, you will become familiar with the following terms:

- ► Ace
- ► Drive Serve
- ► Jam Serve
- ► Lob Serve
- ► Z-Serve

The only time you can score (USRA rules) is when you are serving; thus, mastery of the service is critical for success. According to studies at the Olympic Training Center in Colorado Springs, 27 percent of all rallies are won on the serve. This means that the serve is either an **ace** (no return) or it brings forth an extremely weak return, permitting the server to finish the rally.

There are three basic types of serves: (1) the **drive serve,** (2) the **lob serve** and (3) the **Z-serve.** It is important to not only master the basics of each of these serves but also develop variations for each serve. Variations include different speeds and different heights, as well as serving from different locations in the service box.

THE DRIVE SERVE

The basic drive serve pattern is diagrammed in Figure 7-1. The typical starting foot position for the drive serve is shown in Figure 7-2. Notice that the first step forward is with the back right foot (Figure 7-3). The distance of this step will vary among players but shouldn't be so long as to result in a foot fault (foot going completely over front line of service line) after the next step. The second step is a crossover step with the left foot (Figure 7-4). Keep in mind that you may step on but not over the front service line (Figure 7-5). This crossover forward movement creates the momentum and leverage required to produce power. A proper follow-through is always essential for the correct stroke (Figure 7-6).

THE SWING

The swing used for the drive serve is the same basic stroke as described for the forehand. The point of contact with the ball should be low enough (about knee-high; see Figure 7-7) so that the ball will rebound from the wall and hit just behind the short line. Normally the area in the front which you should aim for is 18 to 20 inches above the floor. This, of course, will vary according to the speed the ball is hit. A good way to determine the proper location on the front wall is to practice a number of drive serves and have a partner mark the spot on the front wall for each serve. Vary the height and location until you hit a perfect drive serve. Visualize this location on future drive serves.

PRACTICE

Drive serves should be practiced to both the left and the right side of the court. For forehand drive serves (right side) you normally aim to hit the front wall about 6 to 8 inches higher than for the backhand serve. To achieve the proper angle you want to maintain the same stroke as for the backhand (left side) serve but drop the ball deeper in your stance.

AIM

In all drive serves the ball should bounce twice before reaching the back wall. Although many instructors teach students to aim the ball toward the corners, it is actually better to aim to hit the ball about 2 feet from the back wall and into the

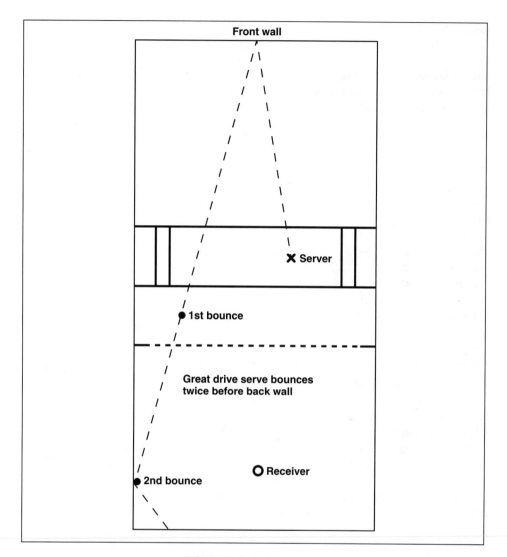

FIGURE 7-1 Drive serve.

▶ **Ace**
A serve that cannot be returned.

▶ **Drive Serve**
A low, hard-hit offensive serve.

▶ **Lob Serve**
A high, softly hit serve that is usually safe.

▶ **Z-Serve**
A serve that hits the front wall then the side wall, bounces, and then hits the side wall again.

FIGURE 7-2

FIGURE 7-3

FIGURE 7-4

FIGURE 7-5

FIGURE 7-6

FIGURE 7-7

side wall (Figure 7-8). Your goal is to make the receiver reach as far as possible. By aiming 2 feet from the back, you cause the receiver to reach 8 to 12 inches farther.

Another benefit of aiming toward the side wall is that if your serve does bounce off the wall before bouncing the second time, it comes off at a deep angle, thus forcing a very difficult return. You always want to make sure your serve does not come off the back wall before bouncing the second time. This serve will always result in an easy setup for your opponent.

As mentioned earlier, you want to practice your serves from different locations. There are three basic service box locations from which to hit your drive serves: the

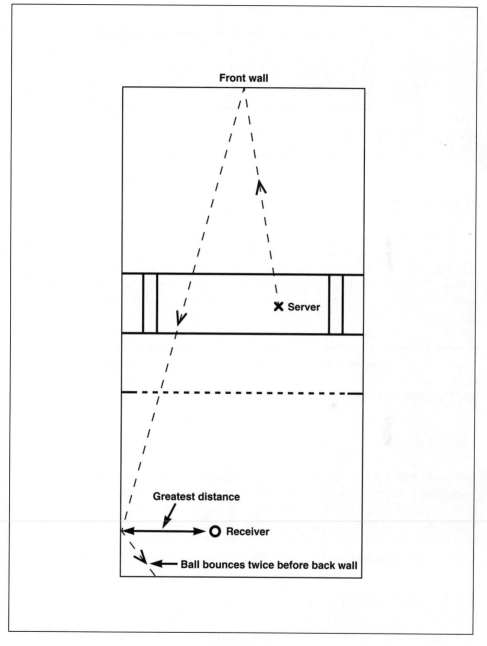

FIGURE 7-8

center, the left side, and the right side (Figure 7-9). Again, you will have to practice from each location to determine the proper angle and height for your serve.

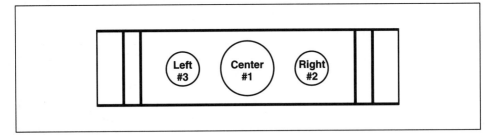

FIGURE 7-9 Service box locations.

JAM SERVE

The **jam serve** is a "trick" serve which tries to catch your opponent off guard. To set up the jam serve, you must establish your drive serve first. After your drive serve has been established and the receiver has become accustomed to your motion for this serve, in all probability he or she will begin to "cheat" by moving to the ball slightly upon seeing your drive serve motion. This is the time to use the jam serve.

The jam serve uses the same forehand drive serve motion except that the aim is slightly higher on the front wall and the shot is angled to hit the side wall about 2 feet behind the receiving line (Figure 7-10). The object of the serve is to bounce the ball off the side wall directly into the receiver's feet. If the receiver is "cheating," the serve will jam into the receiver's body, causing a weak or missed return.

LOB SERVE

A good lob serve is one of the most effective serves you can incorporate into your games. Although lob serves are frequently used for second serves, because of the low risk of a fault serve, they are also effective as first serves. A good lob serve will normally cause the receiver to strike the ball out of his power zone (knee-to-waist area), thus forcing a weak or defensive return. There are three basic types of lob serves: (1) the high lob serve, (2) the lob angle serve, and (3) the half lob serve.

HIGH LOB SERVES

All lob serves should be hit with a controlled, stiff wrist stroke. The ball bounce is higher, allowing the server to strike the ball above the waist.

For the high lob serve you should aim for a spot about 3 to 5 feet down from the ceiling. The ball should bounce just before the 5-foot receiving line and be angled so as to land close to the far left corner (Figure 7-11). In more advanced play the receiver will attempt to cut off the lob service as soon as it bounces. For this reason it is important to have enough height on your lob serve so it will land about 12 to

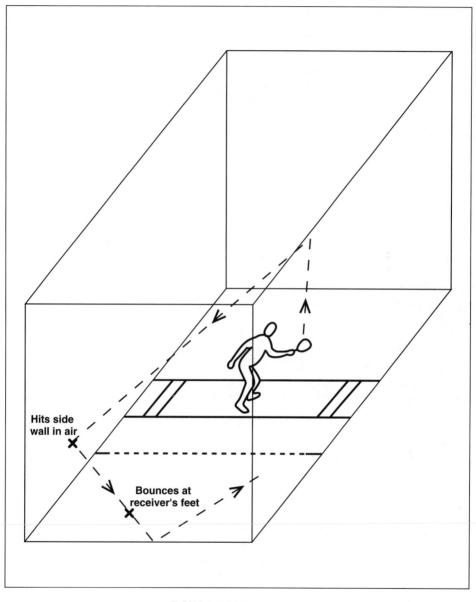

FIGURE 7-10 Jam serve.

► **Jam Serve**

A serve that rebounds off the side wall directly into the receiver.

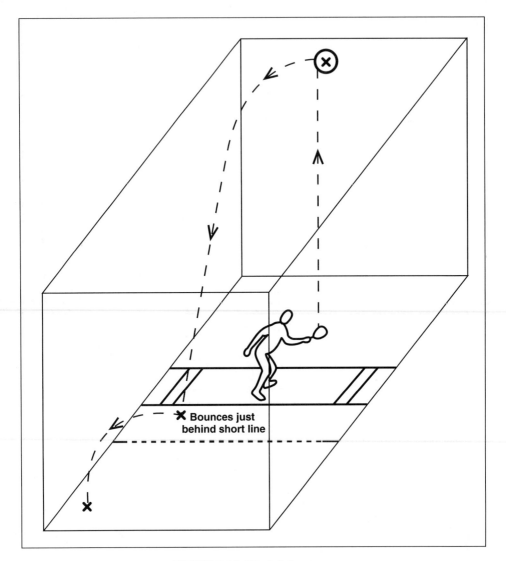

FIGURE 7-11 High lob serve.

16 inches before the receiving line and bounce high enough to force a difficult short-hop return.

LOB ANGLE SERVE

The lob angle serve is becoming the serve of choice for one-serve games. The serve is angled so as to hit the side wall about waist high, 4 feet or so from the back wall (Figure 7-12). This eliminates the opportunity for the receiver to short-hop the ball and also forces the receiver, if he or she decides to make an

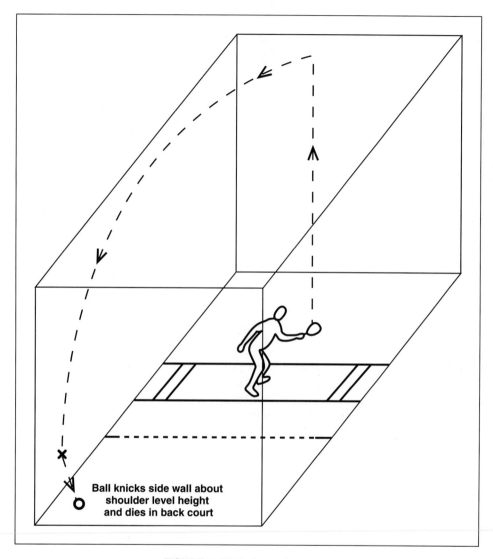

Ball knicks side wall about
shoulder level height
and dies in back court

FIGURE 7-12 Lob angle serve.

offensive shot, to shoot from deep in the court. This is an effective serve to both
sides of the court.

HALF LOB SERVE

The half lob serve is hit about 10 feet high on the front wall. The ball can be hit at
different speeds depending on the height you contact the ball. The ball should
bounce about 1 1/2 to 2 feet from the receiving line (Figure 7-13). Although this
serve seems easier to short-hop, in reality because it is hit harder, the ball reaches

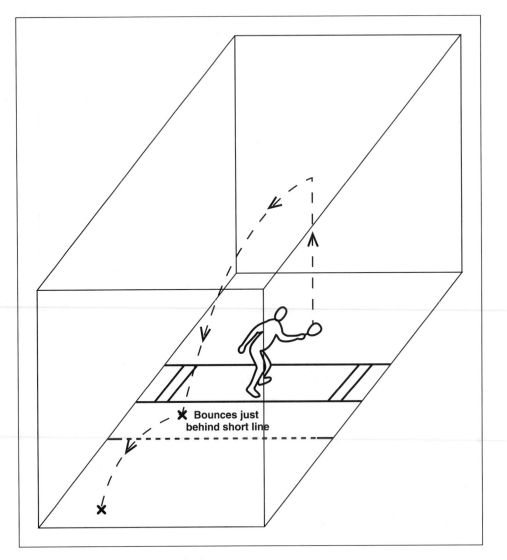

✗ Bounces just behind short line

FIGURE 7-13 Half lob serve.

the receiver faster, and thus it is more difficult for the receiver to achieve proper positioning for a proper short-hop return. The object of the serve is to force the receiver to return the ball at chest level or higher. The ball maintains a more constant height throughout its trajectory as compared to the high lob serve.

Z-SERVE

The Z-serve may be served to the left or right side of the court. Hit high, the serve may be used as a relatively safe second serve forcing a defensive return. Hit

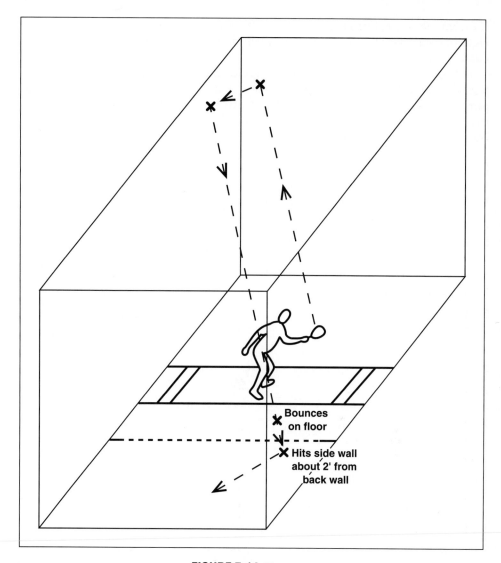

Bounces
on floor

Hits side wall
about 2' from
back wall

FIGURE 7-14 Z-serve.

low and hard, the Z-serve may be used as a first serve, as a deceptive serve trying to catch the receiver leaning in the opposite direction.

The Z-serve is hit from one side of the court toward the opposite corner about 2 feet from the corner seam. The ball then rebounds to the side and travels back across the service box to the opposite rear corner. For the high lob Z-serve, the ball should hit about 2 feet from the ceiling (Figure 7-14), bounce somewhere close to the 5-foot receiving line, and hit the side wall about 2 feet from the back wall about shoulder height or above.

When preparing to hit the Z-serve from the left side, face the corner seam of the front wall and step slightly toward the seam. Z-serves to the forehand side can be hit from many locations starting from the center court. As you move toward the right in the service box you will have to slightly adjust your angle and front-wall contact spot.

The hard Z-serve from the center service location to the right side (forehand for RH) (Figure 7-15) is a good serve to use for deception since it can be hit with almost the same motion as the forehand drive—the only difference is that you drop the ball a little farther ahead in your stance. (Refer to Table 7-1 for an overview of serving strategies.)

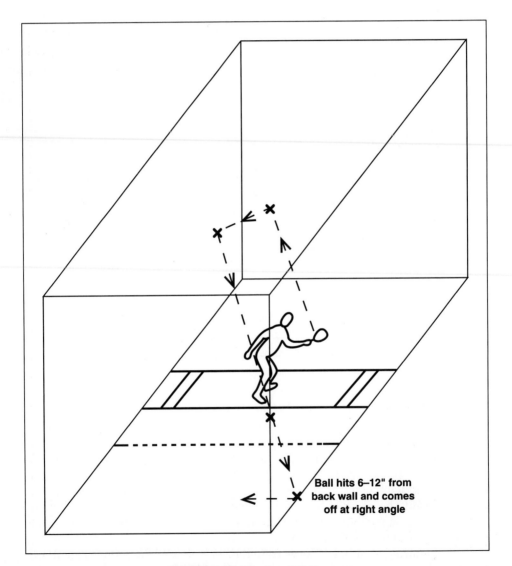

Ball hits 6–12" from back wall and comes off at right angle

FIGURE 7-15 The hard Z-Serve.

TABLE 7-1
Serving: A Strategic Outline

Serve	Target Area		Height of Ball on Contact	Velocity of Ball	Difficulty Level	Difficulty Returning	Start Position (See Figure 7-9)
	Height on Front Wall	1st Bounce					
Drive	About 2 feet or lower	Just behind short line	Knee-high	As hard as possible	Medium for expert; high for novice	Medium to high	1 or 2
Jam	About 3–4 feet	After hitting wall, at receiver's feet	Knees or slightly higher	As hard as possible	Low for expert; high for novice	Medium to high	1 or 2
High Lob	15–17 feet	12 to 16 inches before receiving line	Above waist	Low	Medium for expert; high for novice	Low	1, 2, or 3
Lob Angle Serve	15–17 feet	Hit side wall 5–8 feet from back and bounce	Above waist	Low	Medium for expert; high for novice	Medium	1 or 2
Half Lob	8 feet	12–16 inches from receiving line	Chest to shoulders	Medium	Low for expert; medium for novice	Low to medium	1 or 2
High Z	15–17 feet	12–16 inches from receiving line	Above waist	Low to medium	Medium for expert; high for novice	Medium	1 or 2
Low Z	2–4 feet	Just behind short line	Knee-high	Hard	Medium for expert; high for novice	Medium	1 or 2

SUMMARY

- All players should be familiar with the basic serves—drive, lob, and Z.
- There are three variables on most serves—angle, height of ball, and speed.
- A player should learn to serve from different locations in the service box.

CHAPTER 8

PLAYING BASIC SHOTS

After reading this chapter, you should be able to do the following:

- Describe the basic offensive and defensive shots.
- Describe when and how to properly execute the basic shots.

KEY TERMS

While reading this chapter, you will become familiar with the follow-ing terms:

- ► Around-the-Wall Ball
- ► Ceiling Balls
- ► Offensive Shots

- ► Overhead Slams
- ► Passing Shots
- ► Z-Ball

OFFENSIVE SHOT

Offensive shots are used to score points or to force weak returns from your opponent. As the game of racquetball has progressed so have the variety of offensive shots available to the player.

Since the late 1980s the game has become much more offensive, and at the top level approximately 80 to 90 percent of the game is offensive. In order to advance to the top level of play, it is necessary for players to develop a large arsenal of offensive weapons.

Passing shots are one of the most widely used and effective types of offensive shots. Compared to other offensive shots, passing shots allow greater margin of error during the execution of the shot. If the passing shots are too hard and come off the back wall, they still move your opponent out of center court and force him or her to execute from deep court. There are three basic types of passing shots—wide-angle, down-the-line, and cross-court—which will be covered here along with some other basic offensive shots (kill shots, pinch shots, and overhead slams).

WIDE-ANGLE PASS

▶ When to Hit

Wide-angle passes are hit when your opponent is positioned in front of you, to force your opponent to move out of center court, toward the side wall and into deep court.

▶ How to Hit

The wide-angle pass is hit with a level stroke with particular concentration on a complete follow-through and ball contact near the front foot.

▶ Proper Execution

The ball should hit the side wall parallel to where your opponent is standing or near the 5-foot receiving line. The ball should hit the side wall in the air, then bounce once off the sidewall on the floor, with the second bounce occurring near the back wall.

▶ Purpose of Shot

A wide-angle pass has numerous benefits. First, of course, it may achieve a point or side-out if your opponent is unable to reach the ball. Wide-angle shots also keep opponents off balance and force them to leave the center court area. Even if an opponent is able to retrieve the wide-angle shot, very often he or she is forced to

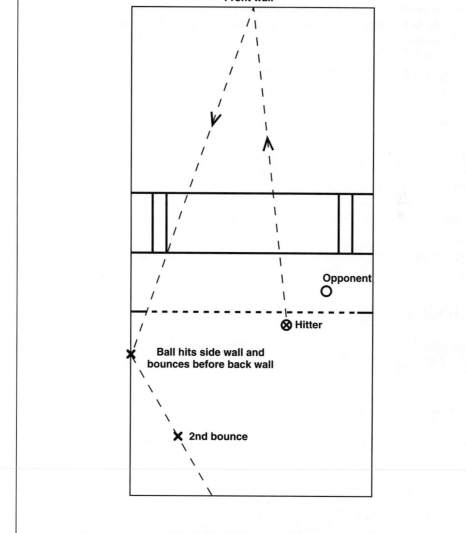

FIGURE 8-1 Wide-angle pass.

▶ **Offensive Shots**
Shots used to win a point or rally.

▶ **Passing Shots**
Shots used to move your opponent out of center court.

return the ball with a defensive shot. Wide-angle passes force the opponent to cover a large area of court, causing long vollies and a great deal of extra effort just to keep the ball in play. The wide-angle pass is a relatively "safe" shot, allowing some degree of error, since it is aimed approximately 2 feet high on the front wall. Even if the wide-angle pass is hit too high or too hard, it still forces your opponent out of center court and requires a deep-court return if played off the back wall.

DOWN-THE-LINE (D-T-L) PASS

▶ When to Hit

The D-T-L pass is hit when you have your opponent trapped on either your left or right side. Your position puts you between the ball and your opponent, forcing your opponent to go around you to retrieve the ball.

▶ How to Hit

The ball is hit to actually bisect the space between you and the side wall. If you square up to the side wall (navel facing the side wall), execution of this shot will be easier.

▶ Proper Execution

When the D-T-L pass is properly executed, the ball should bounce twice before reaching the back wall. If the ball is hit too high, it will rebound off the back wall back to the center court area, leaving a setup for your opponent.

▶ Purpose of Shot

The purpose of the D-T-L pass is to achieve a point or side-out. Although occasionally the shot will force a weak return by forcing your opponent to extend to return the ball, a missed shot in this area—one that is hit too hard or deflects off the side wall—will leave your opponent a setup in the mid-court area. There is less room for error in the D-T-L pass as compared to the wide-angle pass, since missed balls usually end up near midcourt and sometimes even in front court.

CROSS-COURT PASS

▶ When to Hit

The cross-court pass is usually hit when your opponent is in front of you and leaning in one direction or out of position cheating, moving to one side of the court or the other side anticipating your next shot.

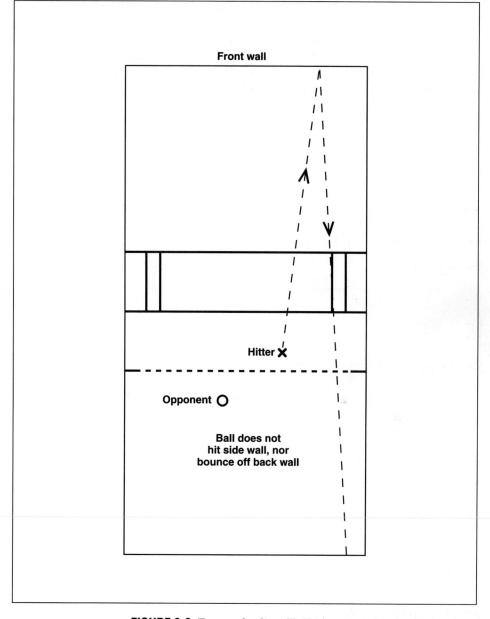

FIGURE 8-2 Down-the-line (D-T-L) pass.

▶ **How to Hit**

The cross-court pass is hit to end up in the opposite corner of the court. Contact point is usually a little farther up in your stance than the D-T-L pass.

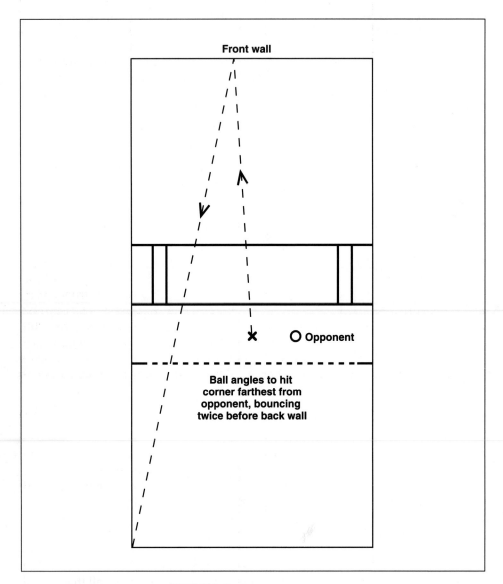

FIGURE 8-3 Cross-court pass.

▶ Proper Execution

When properly executed, the cross-court pass will bounce twice before hitting the back wall. Practice will be required to determine what position on the front wall you should aim at, depending on your court position. If you hit the ball wide, it may bounce back into your opponent, trapping you on the opposite side of the court. If you do not hit the ball wide enough, the ball will rebound off the front directly into your opponent's power area, again trapping you out of position.

▶ **Purpose of Shot**

The purpose of the shot is to drive your opponent out of center court and of course, if possible, win a point or side-out. This shot is easier to hit than the D-T-L pass because of the wider area you have to aim at.

KILL SHOTS

Kill shots are low-percentage shots hit to end the rally. At the lower level of competition, kill shots are normally executed from the service box forward, but at the elite level a kill shot may be hit from any location on the court.

▶ **When to Hit**

You can try a kill shot anytime you feel you have the opportunity and possess the ability to hit the ball so low that your opponent will not be able to return the ball. If you are a lower-level player this may be when you are near the front line of the service box, but if you are an open or upper-level player this may even be when you are 25 feet or deeper in the court. There is little or no room for error with the kill shot. If you hit it too low the ball will skip, and if you hit it too high it may be a setup for your opponent. Because of this, it is important for the shooter to know his or her shot limitations and execute the kill shot only when confident of making the shot.

▶ **How to Hit**

The kill shot is usually made with very low body-to-ball contact. Contact with the ball is normally made at the midcalf area. The ball should be aimed to hit the front wall as low as possible so as to "roll out" or to bounce twice before the front line of the service box.

▶ **Proper Execution**

When this shot is properly executed, the opponent has no chance of returning the ball. A "roll out" occurs when the ball hits so low on the front wall that it does not bounce but simply rolls out flat and there is absolutely no chance for the opponent to return the ball. A kill shot that bounces twice before the opponent can return the ball is hit so low that, even though it bounces, the opponent still cannot return it.

▶ **Purpose of Shot**

A kill shot is the ultimate offensive shot, designed to get a point or side-out. The shot may be hit to rebound back directly at the opponent, but because it is hit so low the opponent cannot return it.

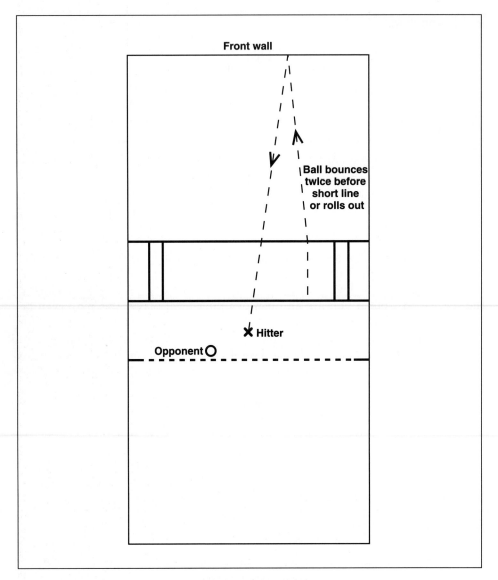

FIGURE 8-4 Kill shots.

PINCH SHOT

A pinch shot is normally hit as an alternate shot to a straight-in kill. Most pinches are hit to win points.

▶ When to Hit

There are a number of situations in which a pinch shot is the best shot to use:

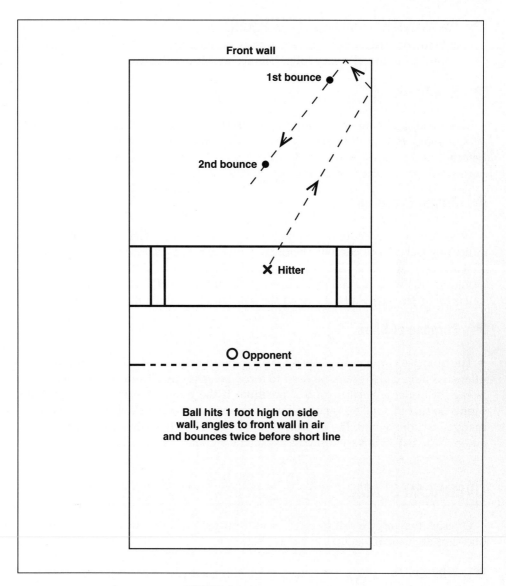

FIGURE 8-5 Pinch shots.

- *When your opponent is in deep court:* Anytime you catch your opponent deep in the court, a pinch shot can be used to force that opponent to travel a long distance in order to retrieve the ball.
- *When you catch your opponent trapped on a side wall:* In this case you want your opponent to travel as far as possible to the opposite side of the court. A properly executed pinch shot will not only force your opponent to travel to the opposite side of the court but also force him to go toward front court, forcing him or her out of the center-court area.

- *When you have a very slow opponent:* Although there may be other shots available to you (such as D-T-L), a properly executed pinch shot will force a slow opponent to travel a very long distance to retrieve the ball.

▶ How to Hit

The pinch shot is hit very similar to a kill shot, with low ball contact. The pinch shot, in many cases, is intended to be a kill shot and either roll out or bounce twice before it gets to the side wall or to the opponent. The pinch shot is hit deeper in your stance than either the cross-court or straight-in D-T-L pass.

▶ Proper Execution

When properly executed, the pinch shot has the same effect as the kill shot—it either rolls out or bounces twice before the opponent can retrieve the ball. The pinch shot should be aimed to hit 1 or 2 feet from the corner on the side wall. If hit too deep along the side wall, the ball may not reach the front wall. Of course, the higher the ball is hit on the side wall the deeper the ball can be hit along the side wall.

▶ Purpose of Shot

The purpose of the pinch shot is to earn a point or side-out. The pinch shot is an offensive shot. It also could be used to force a weak return from an opponent who is caught in deep court or out of position. If the pinch shot is executed a little higher so that the ball does not roll out, the opponent may be able to retrieve it. In many situations where the opponent has to travel a great distance, even if he or she gets the ball, it is very difficult to execute a good offensive shot.

OVERHEAD SLAMS

Overhead slams are hit to force weak returns. Most overheads are returnable and thus are used to set up your next shot.

▶ When to Hit

The overhead is hit to force your opponent out of center court. The overhead is hit as an alternative to hitting a ceiling ball. There are three kinds of overheads you can hit: an overhead kill, an overhead pass, and an overhead pinch. The kill and pinch are intended to roll out in front court or bounce twice before the receiver can get to the ball. The pass is intended to force a defensive return from your opponent.

▶ How to Hit

The overhead is hit from the same position as the ceiling ball. The ball should be above your head in a direct overhand tennis-like manner. The follow-through is complete and down toward the floor. The target on the front wall for the overhead pass is 3 or 4 feet high. The ball may be hit to pass your opponent or hit directly into your opponent's body, forcing a weak defensive return.

▶ Proper Execution

If hit properly, the ball should bounce midway between the front wall and the service line. If the shot is properly executed, the ball should hit the opponent waist-high or above, requiring a defensive return. The second bounce of the ball, if a pass shot, should hit before the back wall. The overhead is a difficult shot to return because of the high bounce of the ball off the front wall. Whereas most other shots are hit with a flat stroke, causing the ball to follow a relatively flat trajectory off the front wall, the overhead is hit with a downward stroke, causing the ball to bounce high.

▶ Purpose of Shot

The purpose of the overhead is to drive your opponent out of center court and either earn a point or a side-out or force a weak defensive return. Many times the overhead is as easy to hit as the ceiling ball, and because it is an offensive shot, it may create more serving opportunities when executed properly. If used as an overhead kill, the shot is usually aimed at the corners, resulting in an overhead pinch. In this case the pinched ball either rolls out or bounces twice before it gets to the side wall.

DEFENSIVE SHOTS

Defensive shots are used to move your opponent out of center court. Most defensive shots are "safe" shots in that they are relatively high-percentage shots that allow the rally to continue. Very often they are strategically used to change the pace of the game and to move your opponent into deep court.

CEILING BALL

Ceiling balls (Figure 8-6) are relatively high percentage shots. Although they are difficult for the beginner because most novices are not used to hitting the

▶ **Overhead Slam**
An offensive shot hit like a tennis serve, rebounding off front wall first and about shoulder level.

▶ **Ceiling Ball**
A defensive shot which hits ceiling and front wall and then bounces high off floor moving opponent to deep court.

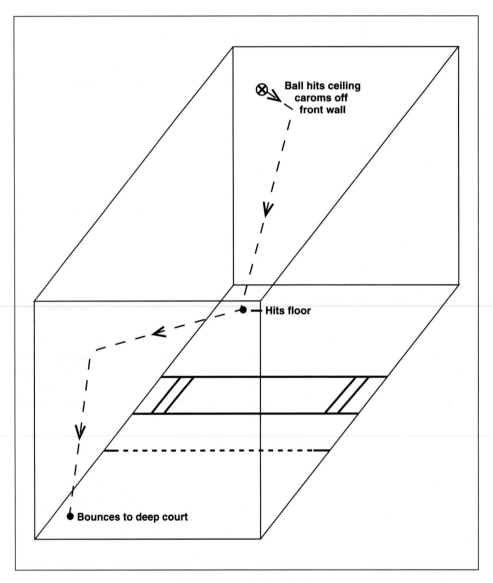

Ball hits ceiling caroms off front wall

Hits floor

Bounces to deep court

FIGURE 8-6 Ceiling ball.

ball above their head, once learned they are an effective shot that every player should be able to use.

▶ When to Hit

Every player needs to develop a consistent defensive game. The ceiling ball is the most widely used defensive shot. It allows you time to recover when out of position. It forces your opponent out of center court, and even if the shot is not hit perfectly, it will still leave your opponent in relatively deep court with a somewhat difficult deep shot. Anytime you find yourself in a position where you cannot hit a good offensive shot, a ceiling ball may be the best alternative. Many players force offensive shots when out of position, especially in the front-court or center-court area; however, in many situations a defensive ceiling ball or around-the-world shot would be a better choice.

▶ **How to Hit**

The *forehand ceiling ball* is hit with an overhand motion. The motion begins with the racquet face facing the ceiling and pointed just behind the head. The arm starts forward with a slight wrist snap followed by a downward follow-through. Similar to its position for other forehand strokes, your body is turned to face the side wall and a step-forward motion accompanies the overhand stroke. The ceiling ball should be aimed to hit the ceiling about 1 or 2 feet from the front-wall-ceiling crotch. Since many factors may affect ball placement (altitude, ball bounciness, force of stroke), players must experiment with proper ball placement. If you need the ball to end up deeper in the court, you must aim closer to the front-wall-ceiling crotch. If your ball is landing too deep, you should aim farther back on the ceiling, thus causing your ball to drop closer to the front wall.

The *backhand ceiling ball* is similar to a forehand ceiling ball in that your swing begins with your racquet behind your head. The racquet comes forward and makes contact with the ball near your front shoulders. Your body is positioned similar to its position for a regular backhand stroke, and your forward step is at a diagonal similar again to the backhand stroke. The follow-through is upward and to the racquet side of your body until the arm is fully extended.

▶ **Proper Execution**

Proper execution of the ceiling ball requires the player to move rapidly into proper position in order to contact the ball in an overhead manner. Proper body positioning and footwork are very important for proper execution of the ceiling ball. Proper swing mechanics are necessary to ensure consistency. The racquet swing should begin at shoulder level, not at the waist. The elbow should lead the swing with wrist snap occurring at ball contact. The follow-through is important to ensure consistent placement and power. When properly executed the ceiling ball will force your opponent out of center court and thus allow you time to get in proper position for the next rally.

▶ **Purpose of Shot**

The ceiling ball is used for a number of reasons. As stated the ceiling ball will force your opponent out of center court. The ceiling ball is a relatively easy shot to execute, and thus it is known as a high-percentage shot. Unlike another type of shot that may be more difficult to execute, such as an overhead smash or an around-the-wall ball, a ceiling ball allows the less-skilled player to utilize a fairly safe defensive shot. The ceiling ball is a good shot to use when your are out of position or off balance. By forcing your opponent into deep court, you are allowed time to recover and regain proper court position. The ceiling ball may be used to frustrate and change the pace of a power player or someone who likes a fast-paced game. By keeping the ball above the power player's waist, you keep the ball out of that person's power zone, thus forcing him or her to either go defensive or hit overhead slams. The ceiling ball is also used as a high-percentage service return. If an offensive opportunity is not available, the ceiling ball again drives the server out of center-court, allowing you to gain center-court advantage. The ceiling ball always will allow you the opportunity to slow down the game and recover if you are tired.

AROUND-THE-WALL BALL

Around-the-wall balls (Figure 8-7) are relatively difficult to hit effectively. There is little room for error, since the ball crosses center court; if hit too soft or too hard, it will set up your opponent.

▶ When to Hit

The around-the-wall ball is a good choice when you want to change the pace of the game or you want to see how your opponent will handle a ball that comes across the court. If your opponent is returning your ceiling balls with good shots and/or is an aggressive player, an around-the-wall shot will change the angle at which your opponent will have to return the ball. If your opponent decides never to cut off the ball as it crosses the center court, then the around-the-wall shot will work as an excellent defensive shot, always moving your opponent to deep court. If your opponent is not good at fly killing (taking the ball out of the air before it bounces) or short-hopping, then the around-the-wall ball will confuse him or her, since he or she will not know whether to cut the ball off in center court or allow it to go to the back wall.

▶ How to Hit

The ball is aimed to hit the opposite side wall about 5 feet from the front-wall crotch and about 15 feet high. The ball then rebounds to the front wall, bounces somewhere in the midcourt area, rebounds to the opposite side wall, and then bounces off the side wall toward the back wall. The ball is usually hit with an overhead swing, similar to that used for the ceiling ball.

▶ Proper Execution

When properly hit, the ball will change direction several times, causing some opponents to be confused. Around-the-world shots can be hit at different heights from mid-side-wall height to very high on the side wall. Variation of these heights

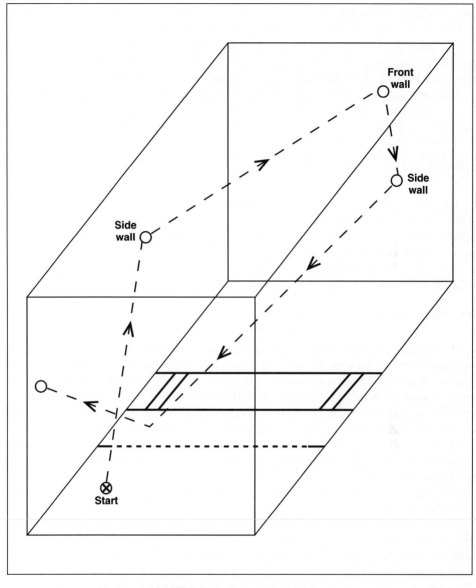

FIGURE 8-7 Around-the-wall ball.

will cause the ball to cross center court at different levels, thus forcing your opponent—if he or she cuts the ball off in center court—to cut the ball off at different heights, a difficult task for most players.

▶ **Around-the-Wall Ball**
A defensive shot hitting side wall, front wall and other side wall, forcing opponent to either cut off or move to deep court.

▶ Purpose of the Shot

The shot may be used to confuse an opponent who has never seen the shot or has been accustomed to normal ceiling-ball rallies. The shot, by changing directions so many times, forces the opponent to retrieve the ball either at midcourt by cutting the ball off, which in many cases is very difficult for many players, or to retreat to deep court and make a difficult offensive shot or another defensive return.

Z-BALL

A **Z-ball** (Figure 8-8) is similar to an around-the-wall ball except that it hits the front wall first and comes off the back side wall at a sharp right angle. This is also a difficult shot to hit safely because if it is hit too short the ball will be an easy setup for your opponent.

▶ When to Hit

The Z-ball is another defensive shot that can be used to confuse your opponent because it hits the wall and comes off at different angles. To hit the ball at the proper angle, you must be positioned at midcourt (somewhere near the short line) or closer to the front wall. If too deep in the court, you will not be able to hit the proper angle (in this case an around-the-wall ball would be a better shot to hit). Since you are in midcourt or front court, the shot can be used to force your opponent into deep court. If you are off balance and unable to hit an effective offensive shot, the Z-ball is an excellent shot to hit. Very often in front court the ball may be hit at waist-to-shoulder height, thus making it difficult to hit an offensive shot. The Z-shot is a relatively easy shot to hit and thus can be used effectively to keep your opponent off balance.

▶ How to Hit

The Z-ball should be hit relatively hard so the ball will take the spin and rebound at right angles in deep court. The ball should be aimed to hit near the opposite front corner about 3 to 4 feet on the front wall. The ball should be aimed at about 13 to 17 feet high. The ball will then rebound to the side wall, across midcourt and into the opposite wall. The speed and angle of the ball will cause it to come off at right angles in deep court. Since the ball rebounds at a right angle in deep court, it is very difficult for your opponent to get the racquet behind the ball; often the only return is to hit the ball into the back wall.

▶ Proper Execution

When properly executed the ball will rebound at a 45-degree angle in deep court, making it very difficult for your opponent to return the shot. The ball must

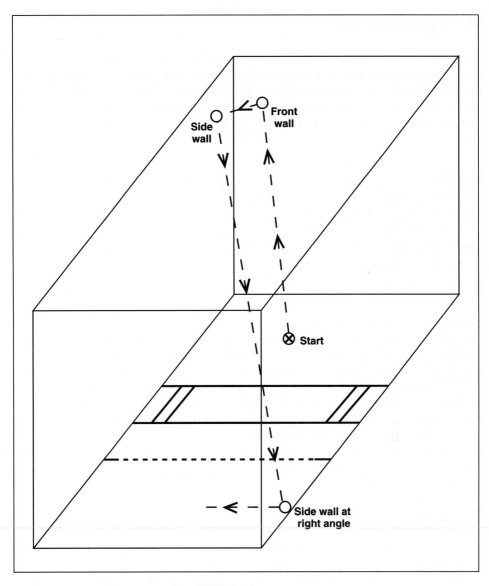

FIGURE 8-8 Z-ball.

be hit from front or midcourt to get the proper angle for the ball to rebound at a 45-degree angle. If the ball is not at the proper angle or with enough speed, it will not rebound at the 45-degree angle. Instead the ball will rebound much like an around-the-wall ball.

► **Z-ball**
A defensive shot, hit to cross the court at a Z angle and move your opponent to deep court.

▶ Purpose of Shot

If you are in the proper court position and either you want to throw your opponent off balance by driving him or her to deep court or the ball is in your high zone (waist-to-shoulder area) and you don't have a great offensive opportunity, then this shot is useful. Sometimes when you are off balance, especially on the backhand side, the Z-shot is an effective defensive shot.

SUMMARY

- Offensive shots are usually used to win rallies and/or points.
- Defensive shots are used to set up your strategy, get your opponent out of center court, and allow you time to prepare for the next rally.
- Players need to practice both offensive and defensive shots in order to use them effectively in game situations.

CHAPTER 9

USING THE BACK WALL

OBJECTIVES

After reading this chapter, you should be able to do the following:

- Describe proper footwork techniques needed to execute the back-wall shot.
- Explain the importance of proper racquet preparation.

KEY TERMS

While reading this chapter, you will become familiar with the following terms:

- ► **Back-Wall Shot**
- ► **Racquet Preparation**
- ► **Side-to-Side Shuffle Step**

   Since the back wall is so frequently used in racquetball, it is necessary for every player to develop efficiency at hitting the ball off the back wall. The stroke mechanics for both the forehand and backhand shots are the same as previously described in Chapter 6. The most important aspect of perfecting a good **back-wall shot** is proper footwork and correct body positioning.

WHEN TO HIT

The back-wall ball is hit anytime the ball comes off the back wall. Many players have a tendency to hit balls above their waist, but if they would just have patience and let the ball drop as it comes off the back wall, in most cases an easier shot could be taken.

Almost any offensive shot may be taken off the back wall. Your opponent's position will help determine which offensive shot should be taken. When executed correctly, the back-wall shot is one of the most effective and high-percentage offensive shots. Since the player's momentum is moving with the ball, the ball may be contacted within the kill zone, and since the opponent's position is known, the back-wall shot permits an excellent offensive opportunity.

HOW TO HIT

Most beginners have a difficult time judging the proper distance between their body and the place for proper ball contact, and also the distance that the ball will bounce off the back wall. The tendency for many players is to go to a spot somewhere 4 to 5 feet from the back wall, plant their feet, and wait for the ball to come to them. This normally results in poor body position, either forcing the player to reach behind for the ball, to reach forward for the ball, or to reach out beyond their normal contact point or else forcing the player to be jammed and thus have to hit the ball in too close.

To avoid these problems the player must develop good footwork techniques to make sure ball contact is made in the proper spot. Proper body position means being in the same position as you would normally be when taking a forehand or backhand shot. Your body is facing the side wall, with your back foot planted (not sliding) and your front foot stepping diagonally into the ball as you hit it. It is important to make sure the ball passes your body before you stroke it. A good way for beginners to learn this skill is to practice without a racquet. Allow the ball to bounce off the back wall and catch the ball with your racquet hand in the spot where correct ball contact should be made. Be sure to allow the ball to travel across your body and make contact near your front foot. This drill forces the player to move his or her body into proper position. To correctly get your body into the right position you must use proper footwork. Back-wall play requires a **side-to-side shuffle step.** The important thing to remember in this step is to not cross your feet over one another. Thus, your back foot slides up to your front foot, and the front foot then slides ahead, with no crossover (see Figures 9-1 through 9-4).

FIGURE 9-1

FIGURE 9-2

FIGURE 9-3

FIGURE 9-4

PROPER EXECUTION

It's important to slide with the ball as it comes off the back wall. To do this the player must follow the ball from the front wall, allow the ball to pass, shuffle-step toward the back wall, and then shuffle-step with the ball as it comes off the back wall, allowing the ball to drop into proper hitting position near the front foot, mid-body area.

Another key to proper ball contact is **racquet preparation** (see Figure 9-1). As soon as the ball passes the player's body en route to the back wall, the player should begin racquet preparation. If the player waits until the ball bounces off the

▶ **Back-Wall Shot**
Any shot that rebounds off the back wall.

▶ **Side-to-Side Shuffle**
The proper way to move your feet when returning a ball off the back wall.

▶ **Racquet Preparation**
An important aspect of back-wall play in which the athlete raises the racquet to its proper position prior to the ball's bouncing off the back wall.

back wall and is passing by the player's body before he or she raises the racquet, very often the player will not be able to execute a proper stroke. In fact, many beginners will hit the ball during racquet preparation as the ball bounces off the back wall, an error easily corrected with earlier racquet preparation.

PURPOSE OF SHOT

Since the ball is moving off the back wall, the player's momentum combined with the ball's momentum can result in a very powerful shot and an excellent offensive opportunity. Continual eye contact is required to follow the ball from the front wall, past the player, off the back wall, and into the player's strike zone. The purpose of the shot is to win a point or end the rally.

SUMMARY

- The back-wall shot is an offensive shot.
- Proper footwork is essential to executing an effective back-wall shot.
- Early racquet preparation and continual eye contact are essential elements for proper back-wall shot execution.

CHAPTER 10

DEVELOPING **STRATEGY**

OBJECTIVES

After reading this chapter, you should be able to do the following:

- Determine the components of a match strategy.
- Describe techniques for scouting opponents.

KEY TERMS

While reading this chapter, you will become familiar with the following terms:

- ► **Advanced Charting**
- ► **Center-Court Area**
- ► **Game Plan**
- ► **Simple Diary**

The components of developing a match strategy are numerous. Although elementary, the basic philosophy of controlling the center-court area is always the foremost strategy any player should implement.

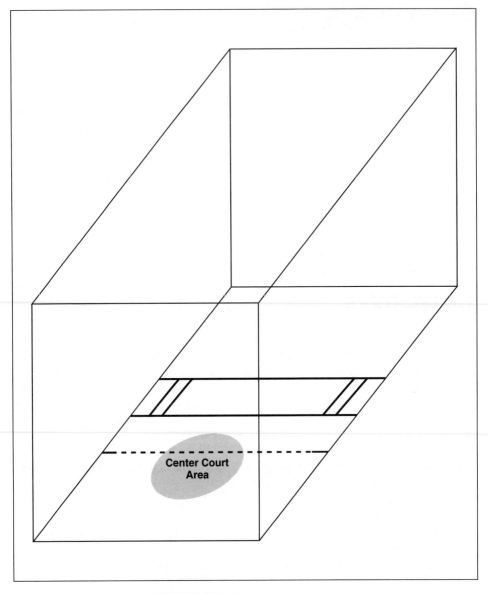

FIGURE 10-1 Center court area.

The **center-court area** is the area immediately behind the safety line (Figure 10-1.) When a player controls this area, which means spending more time in the center-court area than the opponent does, the player usually controls the game. A prime strategy for controlling the area is to hit shots which force your opponent out of the area and then move to the area yourself.

DEVELOPING A GAME PLAN

In developing a **game plan,** you need to consider two major areas:

1. Your strengths and weaknesses
2. Your opponents strengths and weaknesses

Through your training and discussions with your coach or instructor, you should have a fairly good idea of your own strengths and weaknesses. The game plan you develop should concentrate on utilizing your strengths and compensating for your weaknesses. Many racquetball players "learn as they play," or simply play their own strengths, oblivious to the opponent's weaknesses.

As do elite players of other sports, elite racquetball athletes scout their opponents. Although you may not be as sophisticated as a baseball or football scout, you can keep a useful record of the players with which you compete.

SIMPLE DIARY

Many players keep "diaries" or listings of comments on each player they compete against and, in some cases, players they observe playing competitions. When analyzing an opponent, you should observe tendencies during both warm-up and competition. During warm-ups, you can watch your opponent's stroke mechanics to determine such things as where ball contact is made, whether the opponent hits everything off his or her back foot, if the opponent's shot is erratic on the backhand side, and whether the ceiling balls are consistent, along with various other indicators that may assist you in your evaluation. For the most part, if you haven't seen or heard about your opponent prior to the match, then your only opportunity for scouting that opponent is during warm-up.

If you have the opportunity to scout your opponent during another match, here are some questions you'll want to answer:

1. Does the opponent have a weaker backhand or forehand?
2. Is the opponent left-handed or right-handed?
3. Which types of serves are used and which serves are strongest and weakest?
4. Is the serving position always from the same location?
5. Is service return aggressive or defensive?

▶ **Center-Court Area**
The area just behind the service line, which every player should attempt to control.

▶ **Game Plan**
A strategy for winning.

▶ **Simple Diary**
A way of recording basic information about your opponent's strengths and weaknesses.

ANALYSIS OF OPPONENT

Opponent's Name:_____ Date:_____

Other Player's Name:_____ Date:_____

Scores:_____: _____ : _____

Dominant Hand: R L

	Low High Forehand					High Low Backhand			
Power	1	2	3	4	5	1	2	3	4	5
Control/Accuracy	1	2	3	4	5	1	2	3	4	5
Consistency	1	2	3	4	5	1	2	3	4	5

Control player	1	2	3	4	5	Shooter	
Aggressive	1	2	3	4	5	Conservative	
Conditioned	1	2	3	4	5	Tires readily	
Persistent	1	2	3	4	5	Quits	When?
Adjusts	1	2	3	4	5	Rigid	
Confident	1	2	3	4	5	Hesitant	When?
Temperamental	1	2	3	4	5	Calm	
Concentrates	1	2	3	4	5	Loses concentration	When?
Fast game starter	1	2	3	4	5	Slow game starter	

Tendencies/Patterns of Behavior

Sequence of shots relied on: Reactions to certain shots:

Favorite shots/place on court: Reactions to certain setups:

Favorite serves – 1st

2nd

Changes of pace: Common mistakes:

Court coverage: Circumstances:

Summary   Shots   Court Coverage   Tactics

Conditioning

   Weaknesses

   Strengths

Comments: (use the back of the page)

FIGURE 10-2 Analysis worksheet.

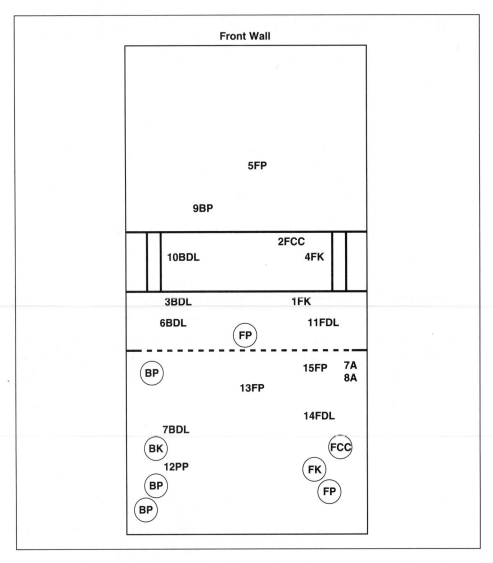

FIGURE 10-3 Advanced scouting system.

6. What are mid-court and front-court tendencies?
7. Are deep-court shot selections low or high percentage?
8. What is the opponent's strongest side?
9. Does the opponent shoot well on the move?
10. Does the opponent like a fast pace or a slow pace?
11. Is the opponent's concentration easily distracted?

The analysis worksheet (Figure 10-2) will help you analyze your opponent. Keep copies of the worksheet in your bag so that at any time you will be able to create a written record of an opponent.

A MORE ADVANCED SCOUTING SYSTEM (CHARTING)

A more **advanced charting** system of scouting normally charts every shot, either every shot during the rally or every serve.

▶ Every Rally

Charting the last shot of each rally will show you exactly what the player tendencies are during the games. This type of charting is often confusing, so we recommend that you chart only one player at a time. The systems and abbreviations used in Figure 10-3, a sample scouting chart, are as follows:

Numbers 1 through 15 indicate points scored.	FP = forehand pinch
A circled abbreviation indicates a shot that skipped.	BDL = backhand down-the-line
BP = backhand pinch	A = ace
FK = forehand kill	FCC = forehand cross-court

From Figure 10-3 you can see that player X is strong from midcourt forward and that deep court is where most of the errors are made. On the backhand side, all skips were made on the pinch shot attempt, while all points were made on down-the-line shots.

After reviewing your charts you can develop a game plan to take advantage of your opponent's weaknesses.

▶ Every Serve

Charting the service simply means recording the position the server begins his serve and what type of serve.

From Figure 10-4 you can determine that the server serves most serves from the center service box position and the backhand drive is the serve used most from this position. The only time the server served to the forehand side was once from the center service position with a 2 serve and all the rest were drive serves from the right service box position. By charting the serve you can determine tendencies and prepare yourself for certain serves. In the example above every time the server moved to the right service box position the receiver should expect a forehand drive serve.

Establishing a game plan against opposing players is only part of developing strategy. Often you will face an opponent whom you have never seen before. Normally, these opponents will fall into one of the categories listed in Table 10-1. The strategies listed are general strategies that will give you some base to determine a tentative game plan. As you play, you can adjust your strategy according to the situation.

▶ **Advanced Charting**
A sophisticated method of recording a player's shots.

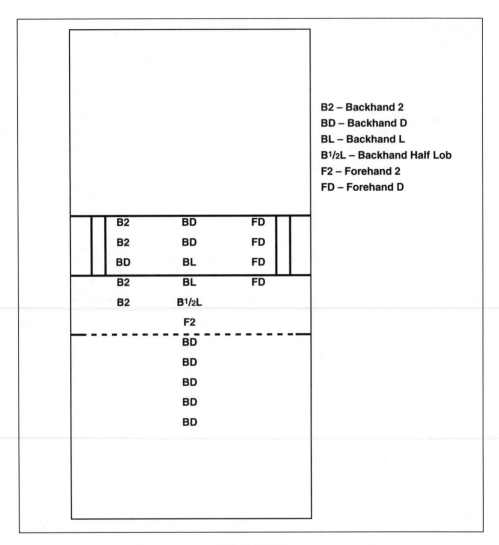

FIGURE 10-4

Table 10-2 provides some strategies that are based on specific game situations.

SUMMARY

- Players need to understand their own strengths and weaknesses.
- Players need to scout or chart opponents in order to develop effective game plans.
- Effective game plans maximize a player's strengths and take advantage of the opponent's weaknesses.

TABLE 10-1
General Strategies to Use Against Unknown Opponents

Opponent's Characteristics	Strategy
Slow, overweight	Get opponent tired; make the player move more than three steps
Quick, good condition	Hit behind; opponent forcing opponent to change directions; slow the game down; roll out when possible
Tall, good reach	Jam (hit into opponent's body)
Short, muscular	Hit out of reach to make opponent stretch
Powerful serves, shooter	Slow down game; place ball above waist; low and hard to backhand
Good forehand, no backhand	Go to forehand with defensive shots only
Aggressive backhand	Lob and soft serves
Great form	Cross-court passes to force opponent to move and hit on the run

TABLE 10-2
Strategies for Specific Game Situations

Game Situation	Strategy
Up 10 to 7	Apply pressure—don't let up.
Down 0 to 7	Hit high-percentage shots—don't force.
Win first game	Start second game with pressure.
Down 14 to 4	Attempt to get momentum; play hard every rally.
Tie breaker 10 to 10 and you are serving	Go with your best and most confident serve. Finish the game when given the chance.

CHAPTER 11

PLAYING DOUBLES

OBJECTIVES

After reading this chapter, you should be able to do the following:

- Describe the different methods of playing doubles.
- Outline the characteristics of compatible doubles teams.

KEY TERMS

While reading this chapter, you will become familiar with the following terms:

- ► Chemistry
- ► Communication
- ► Modified Side-to-Side Method
- ► Side-to-Side Method
- ► Up-and-Back Method

Perhaps the most important aspect in doubles is the ability to select a compatible partner. Although racquetball skill is an important criterion, most often the team that interacts and plays as a team will beat the team that depends on skill alone. A number of factors contribute to a good team, including court coverage, chemistry, and communication.

COURT COVERAGE

The team that covers the court most effectively normally wins. There are three types of positions that are most common in doubles. Coverage in doubles can be attempted by (1) the **up-and-back method,** (2) the **side-to-side method,** and (3) the **modified side-to-side method.**

UP-AND-BACK METHOD

In the up-and-back method (Figure 11-1) the up person covers the front part of the court and the other partner covers the back part of the court. The up-and-back method is the least popular method used in doubles. This method is most effective when one player is extremely quick and is a good retriever and thus can effectively cover the front-court area. The back player must be an excellent shooter, have an effective ceiling game, and also possess equal ability on both sides of the court.

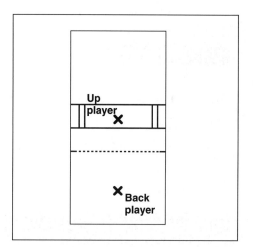

FIGURE 11-1 Up and back method.

▶ **Up-and-Back Method**
A formation in doubles in which one player plays up and one player plays back.

▶ **Side-to-Side Method**
A formation in doubles in which the court is split down the middle with each player responsible for a half.

▶ **Modified Side-to-Side Method**
A formation in doubles where players play half the court, but they also play up and back.

The *advantages* of the up-and-back method are that it puts extra pressure on opponents to make almost perfect shots, compensates for one player's "weak" skills by putting that person in the front-court area, and makes best use of the more skilled player by putting that person in the back court. The *disadvantages* of this method are that it leaves space down the lines, requires greater communication in center-court area, and requires more crossing over among partners in center court, thus creating greater confusion.

SIDE-TO-SIDE METHOD

The side-to-side method (Figure 11-2) is more popular than the up-and-back method. For this method the court is "split" down the middle, and each player is responsible for covering one side of the court. Each player stands about 5 feet in from the side wall and 4 feet behind the short line.

Each player covers both the front and back half of his or her side of the court. The best combination of players for this method of coverage is a strong left side player to play the left side and a strong right side player to cover the right side.

Since the right-side player takes all shots on the right side of the court and vice versa, the only problem arises when shots come in down the middle. With proper communication this problem is easily solved. The side-to-side method is basically a neutral position with both players since neither player is really pressuring the opponents as in the up-and-back method.

The *advantages* of the side-to-side method are that it takes advantage of players' strengths, whether playing on the left side or the right side, and there are fewer communication problems. The *disadvantages* are that it puts less pressure on opponents in front court; if pass shots hit wide there is no one to cover the shot in back court; and each player must be strong on his or her particular side.

MODIFIED SIDE-TO-SIDE METHOD

A more advanced way of playing doubles is the modified side-to-side method (Figures 11-3, 11-4, and 11-5). In this method one player plays "up" around the short line in the middle of one side of the court and the other player plays "back" about 4 or 5 feet behind the short line in the middle of the other side of the court. Although this is similar to the previously described side-by-side method, the difference is that one person is a few feet closer to the front wall and one person a few feet closer to the back wall.

This type of doubles formation is a much more aggressive way of playing doubles than the previous two methods. An example of coverage for this method is shown in Figure 11-5.

In this example player O decides to hit a pinch or down-the-line shot. The up player X1 puts pressure on O by covering the pinch shot, and X2 puts pressure by covering the down-the-line shot.

In this method of doubles, it is possible for the team to adapt and guard against the opponents' strengths and capitalize upon their weaknesses and tendencies. For

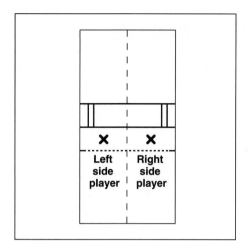

FIGURE 11-2 Side-to-side method.

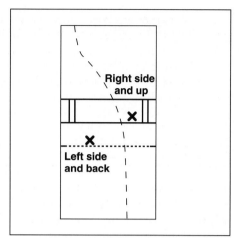

FIGURE 11-3 Modified side-to-side method.

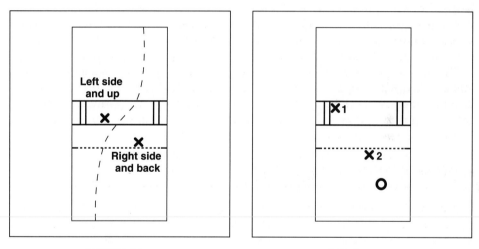

FIGURE 11-4

FIGURE 11-5

instance, in the scenario in Figure 11-5 if player O hits great pass shots and is ineffective at hitting pinch shots, player X1 could move back a few steps to cover the pass shots.

The *advantages* of the modified side-to-side method are that it puts pressure on opponents and takes advantage of opponents' weaknesses. The *disadvantages* are the possibility of overplaying certain shots and the likelihood of allowing execution of certain other shots that cannot be covered well.

OTHER FACTORS AFFECTING DOUBLES TEAMS

Although court coverage is probably the most visible attribute of playing doubles, there are many other factors contributing to a successful doubles team, such as chemistry and communication.

The **chemistry** between partners is vital to a successful doubles team. Chemistry in this case refers to how you feel about your partner. Do you respect your partner? Do you have fun playing with your partner? Do you trust your partner? If the personalities of the partners clash, the players will not work together well. In certain situations, personalities may begin to mesh with time and experience, but it must be remembered that it is not always possible to achieve chemistry with every partner. Chemistry between doubles partners can be seen as a physical and mental relationship. A feeling of oneness must exist between partners, and both players must combine to create one unit.

Communication is another major component of a successful doubles team. Communication is not restricted to game play but also applies to pregame and postgame preparation and analysis. Game strategy is extremely important and must be discussed prior to a match. Both players should be able to discuss strategy and be open to comments from their partner. In order to be successful as a team, the players must share a mutual understanding of what they are trying to accomplish and how they intend to do it.

During the game each person should be aware of shot situation tendencies, court coverage positions, and the general game style that the opposing team will be using. Understanding your partner's tendencies will permit better court coverage during the match. Also, if pregame strategy needs some adjustment during the match, it is important for partners to be able to communicate necessary changes and be cohesive in their new plan.

During rallies it is important for one player to be designated the talker to determine such strategies as who will hit the ball. After the match it is important for players to analyze their strategies and discuss any problems or changes that may be necessary.

SUMMARY

- There are three basic formations for doubles play: (1) up-and-back, (2) side-by-side, and (3) modified side-by-side.
- Communication and chemistry are important characteristics of a successful doubles team.

▶ **Chemistry**
An important attribute of a successful team.

▶ **Communication**
The ability to interact effectively pregame, during the game, and postgame.

NUTRITIONAL
DEMANDS ON THE ATHLETE

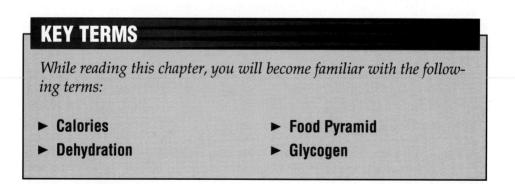

OBJECTIVES

After reading this chapter, you should be able to do the following:

*   Outline the proper nutritional requirements for a racquetball athlete.
*   Explain prematch and postmatch nutritional requirements.

KEY TERMS

While reading this chapter, you will become familiar with the following terms:

► **Calories**   ► **Food Pyramid**
► **Dehydration**   ► **Glycogen**

Proper nutrition is just another factor that the racquetball athlete attempts to control in order to gain an extra advantage. One of the first places an athlete can start to improve upon total performance is *sports nutrition*. What an athlete chooses to eat and drink ultimately affects his or her strengths, timing, and endurance. Input does determine output!

Competitive racquetball athletes need to incorporate proper nutrition into their diets over the entire 12-month training schedule. The proper training diet for racquetball athletes is carbohydrate caloric intake, 70%; protein caloric intake, 12%; and fat, 18%. To ensure proper diet, the racquetball athlete should follow the balanced-diet guidelines presented in the **food pyramid** (Figure 12-1).

PREGAME MEAL

The purpose of the pregame meal is to:
1. Maximize your **glycogen** (carbohydrate) stores
2. Minimize digestion during competition
3. Avoid hunger
4. Provide fluids
5. Avoid gastric distress

Ideally, the pregame meal should be eaten approximately 4 hours before competition. This timing will allow for replenishment of glycogen stores and will allow the stomach to be relatively empty by the time of competition. This is important in order to avoid any gastric discomfort that could arise if food is still being digested. The golden rule for athletes preparing to compete is to eat familiar foods and drink plenty of fluids. The day of competition is not the time to try a new food or diet. Anytime you eat new foods you risk getting gastrointestinal distress such as diarrhea. Another consideration is planning a meal that won't interfere with the physical stress you will put on your body during competition. Racquetball players should eat a precompetition meal that is moderately high in carbohydrate foods— such as bread, potatoes, rice, and pasta—but low in fats. Fluids of choice should also be a part of the meal.

The mental stress that accompanies playing may also influence your stomach. Whether it is physical or mental stress, you will still need to maintain energy and fluid balance to perform your best. Allowing the proper amount of time after a meal before you compete will ensure that your stomach is empty but you are not feeling hungry or weak.

The most important factor to remember about pregame meals is to keep them familiar. If you are unsure about what foods may enhance or hinder your performance, keeping a diary may prove to be helpful. Simply record the amounts and types of foods you eat, when they are consumed, and how you felt before, during, and after competition.

NUTRITIONAL CAUSES OF POOR ATHLETIC PERFORMANCE

Two major causes of poor athletic performance are dehydration and carbohydrate depletion.

The food triangle

As a competitive racquetball athlete, you need to incorporate proper nutrition into your diet over the entire 12 month training schedule.

1 serving
fats, sugar

Protein (6-9 oz.) | Low-fat dairy (2-4 servings)

Vegetables (3-5 servings) | Fresh fruits (2-4 servings)

9-11 servings of breads (grains, pasta, cereal)

Daily caloric intake by food type

% of total calories
Carbohydrates 70%
Fat 15%
Protein 15%

All athletes need these amounts of food on a daily basis!

TRAINING DIET: GUIDELINES TO ENSURE ADEQUATE INTAKE

Food group	Child athlete	Teen athlete	Adult athlete	Professional athlete
Dairy (approx. 90 to 250 calories/serving)	3	4	2	3
1 cup milk, yogurt				
1 oz. cheese				
1/2 cup ice milk, frozen yogurt				
1/2 cup cottage cheese				
Meat, fish, poultry, nuts, cheeses (approx. 200 calories/serving)	2	2	2	4
3 oz. cooked lean meat, fish, poultry*				
2 eggs (or 1 egg plus 2 whites)				
2 oz. cheese				
1 cup dried peas or beans				
2 tbls. peanut butter				
Fruits-vegetables (approx. 60 calories/serving)	6	8	8	12
1/2 cup cooked vegetable/fruit or juice				
1/2 cup raw vegetable/fruit				
1 medium piece fruit				
1/4 cup dried fruit				
Grain, bread, pasta, cereal, beans (approx. 80 calories/serving)	6-8	8-10	8-10	24
1 slice bread				
1/2 bagel, roll, pita, muffin				
1 oz. ready-to-eat cereal (3/4 to 1 cup)				
1/2 cup cooked cereal				
1/2 cup pasta, rice				
1 small potato				
Fluids:	10 to 12	10+	10+	12+
8 oz. water,				
caffeine-free drinks, fruit juice				

Other foods: Select these foods if you need additional calories after you've met the recommended number of servings from the four food groups: Cookies-fig bars, oatmeal raisin cookies, angel food cake, margarine, light salad dressings, popcorn, pretzels.

* Think of this amount as the size of a deck of cards.

FIGURE 12-1 Food pyramid and training diet guidelines.

▶ **Food Pyramid**

An illustration of proper nutritional requirements.

▶ **Glycogen**

The form in which carbohydrates are stored in the body as energy resources.

Pregame Breakfast Menus

#1   1 cup fresh fruit or juice
1 cup cold cereal (Shredded Wheat, All-Bran, Total, etc.) or hot cereal (oatmeal, Cream of Wheat, etc.) plus 2% low-fat milk
fruit juice, water, tea, coffee
    Note: stay away from large amounts of dairy products as they are hard to digest and are high in fat.

#2   1 cup fresh fruit or juice
3 pancakes with "lite" syrup
fruit juice, water, tea, coffee

#3   1 cup fresh fruit or juice
1 choice of bran muffins, whole-grain breads, bagels, etc. (no cream cheese or rich sauces)
fruit juice, water, tea, coffee

Pregame Lunches

#1   pasta (spaghetti, macaroni, etc.)
sauces: tomato or "lite" sauces
fresh green salad or steamed vegetables
bread
fruit, granola cookies
water, juice, tea

#2   vegetable soup or clear soup (not too heavy or rich and creamy)
sandwich: whole-wheat bread, rolls, buns with tuna, chicken, cheese, tomato, and cucumber (no luncheon meats)
fresh fruit
water, juice, tea

#3   vegetarian pizza, cold pasta, vegetarian subs, etc. Create your own lunch menu—just think low in fat, low in protein, and high in complex carbohydrates.

Pregame Meal Reminders

1. Don't miss breakfast; you need to feed your muscles and your mind. Complex carbohydrates are your energy source.
2. Stay away from fatty substances (oils, butter, cream sauces, etc.). Also, do not eat fried foods, because they are too hard to digest.
3. Eat foods that are high in fiber and low in sugar.
4. Drink lots of water.
5. Eat your pregame meal about 4 hours before the match.
6. Don't fast the morning of the game—your muscles need to be refreshed with energy stores of glycogen.
7. If you drink coffee or tea, have it 1 to 2 hours before the match. Do not have more than two cups because caffeine dehydrates your body and the stimulating effect could upset your timing.
8. Do not eat chocolate bars or sweets right before a game because such foods rob you of your water supply, and a prolonged low follows a sugar high.
9. Listen to your body and eat what feels right for you!

▶ Dehydration

The primary nutritional cause of poor racquetball performance over prolonged matches is usually **dehydration.** During exercise, plasma (blood) volume decreases as a consequence of both an increase in sweating and a net movement of water away from the blood vessels.

During a racquetball match you need to remain hydrated. Racquetball athletes should follow the formula shown in the box on top of pg. 106 for the amount of liquids they should consume.

Water has long been considered to be the number one drink for racquetball players. If you are playing only one match and are not worried about other tournament matches the next day, then water may be sufficient. However, some current findings may encourage you to consider a sports drink.

- Cool (5 to 15 degrees °C or 40 to 60 degrees °F) flavored water is voluntarily ingested in greater quantities than is plain water. Therefore, for most exercise, especially racquetball, cool flavored water is the optimal beverage for consumption both before and during the event.
- The addition of small amounts of glucose and sodium to a nutrient beverage (as in sports

▶ **Dehydration**
Lack of liquid, a primary cause of poor performance.

One-Half of Body Weight (in Pounds) = Number of Ounces of Liquid Required per Day

An athlete needs one half of the numerical value of his or her body weight (in pounds) in ounces of water per day to maintain performance. For example, a 175-pound athlete would need 87 ounces of liquid or 8 to 10 glasses of water a day.

drinks) increases the net water absorption and thereby helps to maintain plasma (blood) volume.

- Carbohydrates added to a beverage consumed during prolonged exercise help to maintain blood glucose and thereby delay fatigue in exhaustive efforts (important in tournaments in which players play multiple matches).
- Post exercise consumption of a beverage containing both carbohydrates and electrolytes speeds the recovery of plasma volume and muscle glycogen. This again is important during tournaments when you play multiple matches over a two or three day period. Racquetball players should attempt to condition their body to take small, frequent amounts of fluid, and also accustom themselves to exercising with some fluid in their stomach.

POSTGAME MEAL

During a racquetball game or match you will deplete much of your glycogen reserves. When you are playing in tournaments it is necessary to replace this lost

Organizing Your Nutritional Liquid Requirements

Day Before Competition

8 ounces with each meal
8 ounces between meals

Pre-Event Meal

16 ounces with meal
6 to 8 ounces every 15 minutes prior to and during match

glycogen in order to prepare for your next match. Glycogen reserves can be replenished within 24 hours after a game if these guidelines are followed:

1. Ingest some form of carbohydrate immediately after exercise (within 20 minutes).
2. Consume 0.3 to 0.7 grams of glucose per pound of body weight every 2 hours during the initial 6-hour postmatch period.
3. Ingest approximately 600 grams of carbohydrates during the 24-hour postexercise period.

HOW MANY CALORIES DOES A RACQUETBALL PLAYER NEED DAILY?

Calories are important to the racquetball athlete because they are an indication of energy consumption and usage. Your caloric requirement is dependent on your age, your body size, and your daily activities. In order to determine how many calories you should be consuming each day, use the following formulas:

Weight x 10 Calories = Basic Metabolic Rate
Add 600 Calories for each hour of training or play. For example,

$$
\begin{array}{ll}
170 \text{ pounds} \times 10 \text{ calories} & = 1{,}700 \text{ calories} \\
2 \text{ hours of racquetball} & = \underline{1{,}200 \text{ calories}} \\
& 2{,}900 \text{ calories per day}
\end{array}
$$

SUMMARY

- Adequate carbohydrate consumption and hydration are important nutritional requirements for proper racquetball performance.
- Pregame meals should consist of familiar foods and should be eaten about 4 hours before the match.
- Postgame nutrition should replenish depleted glycogen reserves and rehydrate the athlete.

▶ **Calories**
An indication of energy consumption.

CHAPTER 13

CONDITIONING FOR
RACQUETBALL

OBJECTIVES

After reading this chapter, you should be able to do the following:

- Outline the basic requirements of a 12-month training schedule.
- Explain the basics of aerobic, anaerobic, and plyometric training.

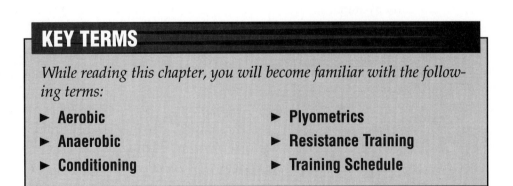

KEY TERMS

While reading this chapter, you will become familiar with the following terms:

▶ Aerobic

▶ Anaerobic

▶ Conditioning

▶ Plyometrics

▶ Resistance Training

▶ Training Schedule

When developing a racquetball conditioning schedule, many different factors must be taken into consideration. Racquetball is much more than just proper stroke execution and mental preparation. To maximize his or her potential the racquetball player must incorporate other facets of **conditioning** such as weight training, speed training, anaerobic and aerobic conditioning, and, of course, proper stretching.

Like many other sports, racquetball has developed to the point where proper conditioning plays a major factor in an athlete's success. To implement the various aspects of conditioning, the development of a **training schedule** is key. Proper preparation requires a systematic approach to conditioning. Each aspect of conditioning requires a concentrated training period to fully develop each area.

When planning your conditioning schedule, you will probably want to peak for certain events. Research indicates that an athlete can only reach a peak performance level for a maximum of 2 or 3 weeks, making it important for athletes to schedule their training and conditioning so as to enable them to peak for the most important competitions.

All serious athletes *plan their play and play their plan.* Once you determine your peak events and your training schedule, it is important that you follow your plan. Periodic adjustments may be made to include new events and to attend to personal schedules, but every effort should be made to maintain the overall plan.

To coincide with the training schedule presented in the appendix, we will divide the conditioning schedule presented here into four phases:

1. Introductory phase
2. Strength phase
3. Power phase
4. Maintenance phase

The athlete can divide the phases into any length of time desired. Some athletes may want to divide their schedules into two 6-month periods, while others may want to concentrate on a 12-month schedule. To maximize the training effect of each phase, each phase should be at least 6 weeks in length.

RESISTANCE TRAINING

Resistance training has been shown to reduce injuries, delay the onset of fatigue, and improve performance in most athletes.

▶ **Conditioning**
A general term incorporating various aspects of training to properly prepare the athlete for competition.

▶ **Training Schedule**
The organization of training regimes over a specified period of time.

▶ **Resistance Training**
A type of training which requires the body's musculature to move against some type of opposing force.

PHASE I: INTRODUCTORY PHASE

This phase should be designed to orient the player who is unfamiliar with weight-training techniques and to prepare that person for the next phase of training. In this phase the athlete should do a high number of repetitions with little weight. This approach will condition the athlete for greater workloads later.

PHASE II: STRENGTH PHASE

Strength is a key ingredient in any sport. Racquetball requires that you have a firm grip throughout your stroke. Many stroke problems occur because an athlete releases the grip at contact time. Strength in your hips and legs is needed for quick lateral, forward, and backward movements. The exercises performed in this phase isolate the muscles involved in racquetball in order to attain the strength needed to compete.

In the strength phase the sets and repetitions are decreased while the weight is increased. The rest periods are longer to assure that the muscle worked is allowed to nearly recover between sets. This approach enables the athlete to perform the exercises with heavy resistances, which create maximal gain in strength.

PHASE III: POWER PHASE

During this phase the exercises become more sport-specific as they work on the development of power for the competition season. Multiple joint exercises focus on attaining the explosive power needed for success in racquetball. Power may be translated into the athlete's ability to move his or her body from one position to another very quickly and to hit the ball with normal velocity.

PHASE IV: MAINTENANCE PHASE

Maintaining the benefits of power and strength over the entire competition season is of great benefit to the racquetball player. A conditioned player will usually recover more quickly, have fewer injuries, and play a better game than a nonconditioned player. This phase is designed to maintain the benefits developed earlier in the season while at the same time getting the athlete in and out of the gym quickly so as to allow more time for practicing racquetball-specific skills.

AEROBIC CONDITIONING

Although racquetball seems to be strictly an **anaerobic** sport (a sport involving short, explosive bursts of energy, causing a fluctuating heart rate), research at the Olympic Training Center has produced some interesting results. Outfitted with heart monitors, athletes participating in the research played under simulated tournament conditions. Somewhat surprisingly, these athletes exhibited little fluctuation of heart rates. In fact, heart rates quickly rose to 70 to 75 percent of maximum and remained at these elevated levels throughout the match, even during the 10- to 15-second breaks between points. This research indicates that a certain level of aerobic conditioning is important for racquetball play.

For players interested in tournament play, the benefits of better conditioning such as faster recovery between matches and more efficient heat dissipation are added reasons for developing a strong **aerobic** base. The important criteria in developing an aerobic training schedule is to elevate the heart rate to 75 to 80 percent of your maximum for at least 20 to 25 minutes two or three times per week.

DETERMINING MAXIMUM HEART RATE

The formula for determining maximum heart rate is:

220 minus your age = (estimated) maximum heart rate in beats per minute (bpm)

Thus, a 40-year-old athlete's estimated maximum heart rate would be 220 minus 40, or 180. The target heart rate for exercising is 80% of maximum heart rate, so for this example it would be 144 bpm. This means that a 40-year-old racquetball player should exercise for 20 to 25 minutes while maintaining his or her heart rate at 144 bpm to obtain some form of aerobic conditioning.

To monitor your heart, take your pulse by placing your index finger on your carotid (neck) artery. Count your heart rate for 10 seconds (beginning at 0) and then multiply by 6 to obtain the rate per minute. Heart rate measurements should be taken immediately after cessation of exercise or by stopping momentarily in the middle of an exercise session.

After doing this a couple of times during your workout, you will become familiar with the pace at which you should be working.

AEROBIC TRAINING

Although it is true that conditioning exercises such as jogging or bicycling will result in development of an aerobic base, for racquetball we suggest a much more sport-specific aerobic routine.

▶ **Anaerobic**
Literally, "without oxygen." In racquetball the term refers to short activity bursts that result in a fluctuating heartrate.

▶ **Aerobic**
Literally "with oxygen." In racquetball, the term refers to conditioning exercises which usually last 20 minutes and are performed at 70 to 75 percent of maximum heart rate.

By incorporating specific speed and agility drills into a 20- to 25-minute continual workout, you can elevate your heart rate to the 75 to 80 percent target zone, thus working toward aerobic fitness while at the same time training your body to react with speed and agility.

Caution: At first, monitor your heart rate often to make sure it is not too low or too high. Too low means you are getting no aerobic benefit, whereas too high means your body is working anaerobically.

SKIPPING

Training aerobically has continually referred to exercises such as running, bicycling, and swimming. For racquetball, a more defined and applicable aerobic training schedule is recommended.

Since racquetball requires rapid movements in conjunction with conditioning, a combination of various skipping exercises designed for warm-up performed over a 20-minute period combines the benefits of speed training with aerobic training.

The following exercises will not only warm up your body but will also help you move your feet more quickly. Set up a distance equal to the distance between the front wall and back wall of the court. The skipping is done to a right-right-left-left rhythm. Start by practicing the movement standing still and then repeat the movement while skipping. This will help you get used to the movement, stretch your muscles, and focus on movement mechanics. After you are comfortable with the movement, try some of these variations:

Initial movement: Standing
5–10 each side

Straight ahead skip: (1 time)

Toe taps: Point toe up-down-up-down . . ., switch feet.

Step over: Foot moves back, up, and over the knee in a circular pattern.

Knee hugs: Lift knee to chest, wrap arms around knee, pull knee to chest.

Reach back: Facing backward, lift the knee up and reach back with the heel, then down.

Karate kick: Knee up, reach out with the heel.

Open drop step: Facing backwards, bring knee up, out, and back. Keep shoulders pointed.

Secondary movement: Skipping
10–15 yards

Ankle flip: Skip from the balls of your feet with legs straight.

Step over skip: Same foot pattern as standing-toe up, knee up, heel up.

High knee skip: Lift knee as high as possible.

Backwards skip: Skip backward bring knee up and reach back with the heel.

Karate kick skip: Toes pointed up.

Open drop step skip: Quick rotation of the hips.

Crossover step: Facing sideways, knee up and across the body in one movement.

Hands close to pockets: Arms "run" in place.

Big leg circles: Keep legs straight and bring foot above hip region.

Crossover skip: Quick rotation of hips with an explosive crossover.

Quick skip: While feet gradually get faster. Fast arms swings.

Circle skips: Emphasis on big leg circles, foot above hip region.

INCORPORATING AEROBIC TRAINING INTO YOUR PHASES

▶ Phase I

The development of an aerobic base should take place during this phase. Since the athlete is not concentrating on racquetball skills, this is a good time to develop the physical conditioning aspects required for peak performance. Many athletes require a time away from the game, so this phase allows for such a break while still developing skills required for peak performance.

▶ Phase II, III, IV

When the athlete develops an aerobic base, it is relatively easy to maintain the conditioning effects by working out twice a week for 20 to 25 minutes. This is the time when a schedule of speed skills performed over the designated time period embraces the benefits of both aerobic training and speed training.

ANAEROBIC TRAINING

Racquetball requires speed and rapid movements. Much of what is described regarding speed and agility training is also known as plyometric training. **Plyometrics** is a training principle using explosive calisthenic-like exercise to develop power. Power is a combination of speed and strength. While resistance training (weight lifting) is designed primarily to increase strength, plyometrics is most effective at improving the speed component. The most effective way to increase power is with a combined program of resistance training and plyometric training. Racquetball players use explosive movements to hit the ball and quickly take the first step to retrieve the ball. Thus, you must train for lower-body speed and agility and for upper-body explosive movement. Since plyometrics involves such an intensive form of training, certain precautions must be taken before incorporating speed/agility drills into your training.

▶ Plyometrics
An intensive form of training using explosive exercises to develop power.

PLYOMETRIC TRAINING GUIDELINES

1. Plyometric drills must be done on an appropriate surface. If the surface is too hard, the possibility for injury increases.
2. Athletes must wear appropriate shoes (court shoes) when performing plyometric training.
3. The athlete must have an adequate strength base before initiating a plyometric training program.
4. Because of the high intensity of plyometric training, adequate rest periods must be taken. Rest periods should be of adequate duration between sets and exercises to remove any feeling of fatigue (approximately 2 minutes).
5. Plyometric training should be progressive in nature, both in terms of volume and intensity.

Plyometric training should be initiated at the end of Phase II, after your strength base has been developed. In Phase II you should concentrate on lower-body speed/agility plyometric-type exercise. In Phase III you should concentrate on upper-body explosive movements.

PLYOMETRIC TRAINING FOR RACQUETBALL

▶ Mini-Hurdles

The recommended number of hurdles is 10. Place the hurdles in a straight line unless the drill specifies a different configuration. Note that mini-hurdles help your lift mechanics, so make sure you are firing the knee up, not just lifting the foot over the hurdle. Here are some mini-hurdle drills to try:

1. One Leg: Place hurdles one yard apart. One leg "hurdles" and the other is on the outside. The outside leg stays straight, while the moving leg cycles up and over the hurdle (Figure 13-1).
2. Two Steps: Place hurdles one yard apart. Similar to running in place, two feet over each hurdle. This is an aggressive sprint through the hurdles focusing on the leg cycle. Do not jump over hurdles—run! (Figure 13-2)

FIGURE 13-1 Mini-hurdles.   **FIGURE 13-2** Mini-hurdles.

3. Two Steps Lateral (Figure 13-3): Place hurdles one yard apart. The front leg moves up and over the hurdle while the back leg is on the outside of the hurdles. There is one touch between each hurdle with the front leg.
4. Front Leg Explosion: Place hurdles one yard apart. The front leg moves up and over the hurdle while the back leg is on the outside of the hurdles. One touch between each hurdle with the front leg.
5. Back Leg Explosion: Place hurdles one yard apart. The back leg moves up and over the hurdle while the front leg is on the outside of the hurdles. There is one touch between each hurdle with the back leg.
6. Lateral Change of Direction: Place hurdles one yard apart. For this drill you need another person. You start in the middle of the hurdles, and the other person points right and left randomly. You must move laterally through the hurdles reacting to the other person's signals.

▶ Ball Drops

Here is a fun drill to help develop first-step explosion and reduce false stepping. You need to be in a service position with a partner about 4 to 5 yards away. Hold out two balls. Drop one ball, and the other athlete must get to the ball before it bounces twice. Adjust the distance to challenge the speed and abilities of each individual. Stay on the front foot.

Here are some variations:

- *Facing forward:* Get into good service position up on the front foot like a cat ready to pounce on a mouse. Don't anticipate—just react to the stimulus. Focus on push; push as you explode for the ball. If you are taking a false step (stepping backwards first), work to get lower in your receive position or start about 6 inches from a wall. This will force you to explode forward.
- *Facing back:* Now focus on the hips and stepping back. Again, concentrate on staying on the front foot and push, push, push. Drop the hip straight back as you explode and go. Don't turn then go—it should be all one motion.
- *Lateral:* Focus on your crossover moves. As the ball is dropped, drive the knee and hip across as you run to get the ball.

▶ Upper-Body Plyometrics

Here are some drills using upper-body plyometrics:

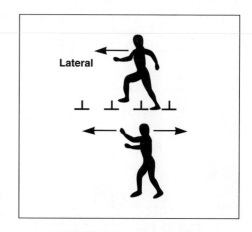

FIGURE 13-3 Lateral drills.

FIGURE 13-4 Ball drops.

FIGURE 13-5

FIGURE 13-6

1. Side Throw (Figures 13-6 and 13-7): This exercise will develop shoulder and hip rotation. Shoulder and hip rotation are extremely important for development of power and fluid stroke mechanics. *Procedure:* Swing the ball as far to the right as possible and then forcefully reverse direction to the left. Toss the ball to a friend or against a court wall.
2. Kneeling Side Throw (Figures 13-8 and 13-9): This exercise isolates hip and shoulder rotation and helps develop follow-through. Reverse the procedure to isolate the other side. *Procedure:* Kneel with ball at waist level. Twist upper body and arms together and throw against wall or to partner.
3. Pullover Pass (Figures 13-10). This exercise works on shoulder, arm, and wrist power. *Procedure:* Lie on back, keep arms extended, and throw ball to partner.

▶ Agility Drills Incorporating Plyometric Principles

The following drills are done in three sets of 10 each, two to three times per week.

- *Jumps:* Focus on keeping both feet on the ground at the same time. Side-to-side: Simply do 10 touches as you jump side to side across the line. Front-to-back: Do 10 touches as you jump forward and then back.

FIGURE 13-7

FIGURE 13-8   FIGURE 13-9

- *Hops:* These are done with one foot at a time. Side-to-side: 10 touches. Front-to-back: Same as jumps.
- *Lateral push drills:* Focus on teaching the body to push with the outside foot. Simply jump side to side, touching the lines with the foot and immediately changing direction. Do this again for 10 touches.
- *Box drills:* Using a 10-inch box, start at the top of the box, jump off. Touch the ground quickly and explosively as you pop off the ground.

FIGURE 13-10

▶ **These are more plyometric skills used to improve agility**

- *First do Jumps:* Both feet at the same time, 10 quick jumps.
- *Next do Hops:* Alternate five with the right five left, five right five left, then rest.
- *Next do Side-to-side:* To work on lateral, push off and quickness.

Start with one foot on the box and one on the ground. Jump to the other side landing with the feet switched from the starting position. Jump over a line and back repetition. Start with both feet apart (as in receiving stance). Jump over line on floor and then back. Concentrate on quickness, popping off the ground, and good body control. Do drill for 30 secs. Rest for 30 secs. Repeat 3 times.

COURT DRILLS FOR POWER AND AGILITY

Speed/agility exercises can also improve your anaerobic conditioning. In Phase III you may want to include more specific racquetball drills emphasizing short

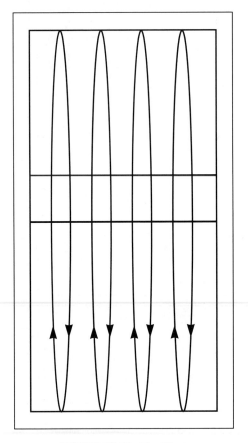

FIGURE 13-11 Shuttles.

bursts of speed and simulated racquetball surges. The following drills not only work on your footwork and anaerobic conditioning but also familiarize you with court dimensions and simulate actual court movements. To add more game-like realism, carry your racquet and complete each movement with a forehand or backhand stroke. Emphasize good stroke mechanics for each swing. For an aerobic workout do the drills at moderate speed, with no rest. For an anaerobic workout do the drills at full speed, and let your resting time be equal to your working time.

1. Shuttles: Players run end to end in the court, always facing the front wall (Figure 13-11).
2. Stars: Players run to each point of the star in sequence, stressing proper footwork (that is, as would be used in a game) for the different directions (Figure 13-12).*
3. Perimeters: Players touch each corner, using proper footwork along each wall (Figure 13-13).

FLEXIBILITY

Stretching is essential to peak performance and injury reduction. As previously described, it is beneficial for athletes to warm up before matches by using a combination of speed drills and ballistic (moving) stretches. By following the warm-up exercises earlier described (in Chapter 13), the athlete will first warm up his or her body to the "sweating" stage and then activate and prepare the muscles for rapid movement.

Stretching is an important but often neglected part of every elite athletes training regime. Stretching reduces the chance of injury, and increases the athletes range of motion. In racquetball you instantly reach for shots, thus range of motion is important.

After the match, static (holding) stretches are beneficial. These are the typical exercises for which the athlete holds a particular stretch for 10 to 15 seconds. These

* All lateral movements would use shuffle step.

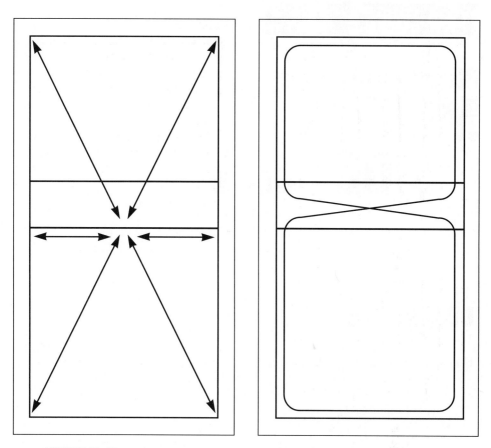

FIGURE 13-12 Star pattern.   **FIGURE 13-13** Perimeter pattern.

exercises help eliminate soreness and prepare the muscles for further activity such as that which occurs during tournaments.

SUMMARY

- In order to maximize his or her training efforts, an athlete must organize the training schedule so he or she can peak for important events.
- A complete training schedule must include resistance training, aerobic and anaerobic training, and speed training.

PREPARING FOR THE
MENTAL
SIDE OF THE GAME

OBJECTIVES

After reading this chapter, you should be able to do the following:

* Describe various techniques for improving mental toughness.

KEY TERMS

While reading this chapter, you will become familiar with the following terms:

► Concentration

► Cue Words

► Eye Control

► Flow State

► Psych-Out Zone

► Psych-Up Zone

► Relaxation

► Rituals

► Self-Talk

► Synergism

► Visualization

One of the most important aspects of preparing for racquetball competition, but often the most overlooked, is mental preparation. Your training and playing will be greatly enhanced if, before you begin a training schedule, you make sure you know all about yourself. There are many psychological and sports-specific profiles athletes can complete to learn more about their strengths and weaknesses. Some of the questions these profiles help answer are the following:

- *Who am I?* It is important to understand your strengths as well as your weaknesses. What are your interests, skills, values, and beliefs as an athlete and as a whole person?
- *What do I want?* What are your dreams and goals, your life purpose? Who and what are important to you and your quest?
- *How can I get there?* Journal on a daily basis. Journaling and charting your growth is necessary to gauge your progress.

THE COMPLETE ATHLETE

The long-accepted model for training athletes has been to work in the areas of psychology, physiology, and sociology. Each area was usually approached separately with little connection between each (Figure 14-1). In reality, most athletes concentrate primarily on the physical aspects of training, for the most part neglecting the psychological and social aspects (Figure 14-2).

In the future, however, athletes will be taught to balance their training regimens (Figure 14-3) and develop **synergism** in their lives. Coaches will stress and alert athletes to take care of themselves and accept the responsibility for achievement or failure.

The law of control in sports says that *the more in control athletes feel about their sports and their lives the better they feel about themselves.* An athlete needs to know what is in his or her control—and what is not!

Within the athlete's control are such things as thoughts, beliefs, attitude, focus, concentration, pregame psyche plan, visualization, relaxation, rituals, strategies, diet, rest, and on-court presence. Out of the athlete's control are opponents, referees, coaches, teammates,

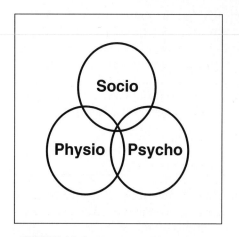

FIGURE 14-1 The complete athlete.

▶ **Synergism**
A balance between training, competition, and personal life.

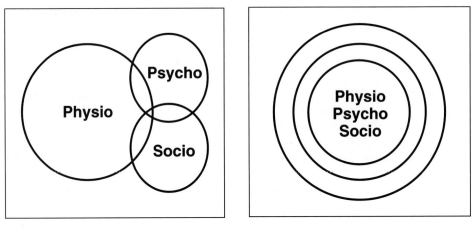

FIGURE 14-2   FIGURE 14-3

linesmen, spectators, sport politics, court conditions, scheduling, seeding, previ-ous rounds, and rallies.

DEVELOPING MENTAL TOUGHNESS

To develop mental toughness in racquetball involves training in a number of disciplines. Mental toughness requires training in self-talk, rituals, concentration, confidence, relaxation, desire and motivation, and visualization.

SELF-TALK

The key to success in sports is having a positive attitude no matter what the sit-uation. Winning is an attitude as much as a physical skill. Positive affirmation, or **self-talk,** is a method of maintaining that winning attitude. A positive affirmation is a personal, positive, and present statement about the way you want to be. It is important when playing racquetball to stay focused, and self-talk is a form of internal dialogue that helps you maintain focus on the task at hand. Example– My drive serve is great, I know I will get a weak return or ace if I use it now!

RITUALS

Another way of developing mental toughness is to determine defined **rituals.** A ritual is a physical action or technique that will bring the mind and body back into its ready state in the present moment. Some examples of on-court rituals:

• Picking and concentrating on strings

- Spinning racquet to keep wrist loose
- Shoulder shrug
- Adjusting headband and glasses
- Breathing deeply to relax and invigorate your body
- Bouncing the ball to get rhythm and tempo

Rituals relax the body, trigger an appropriate neuromuscular response, and bring your "mind into your muscles."

CONCENTRATION

Many people lose games because they become distracted and lose the ability to concentrate during the game. To maintain **concentration,** an athlete must keep his or her mind in the "now." This will mean, at times, that the athlete must empty the mind of past and future thoughts and "become one" with the present moment.

To maintain mental toughness, the athlete must learn to *maintain concentration.* Choking in racquetball occurs when the athlete's mind moves out of the present moment.

PAST	PRESENT	FUTURE
Oh, no!	Now!	What if?

Here are some hints on how to eliminate distractions and maintain concentration.

1. *Practice **eye control**:* One of the major distractions is spectators, as well as other people around the court—even your opponent and the referee. To stop yourself from looking outside the court, concentrate on your racquet strings. If your opponent is complaining to the referee or making distractions, simply focus on your strings. Another way to avoid looking at spectators on glass back walls is to walk backward to the receiving position. This way you never look outside and thus maintain your concentration on the court.

2. *Focus on the ball:* We've all heard the expression "Keep your eye on the ball." A way to help you concentrate on ball contact is say to yourself "Contact!" or

▶ **Self-talk**

The positive way one speaks to oneself during competition.

▶ **Rituals**

A series of predesignated, repeated actions used to develop confidence and consistency.

▶ **Concentration**

The ability to focus on a task.

▶ **Eye Control**

The ability to keep eyes focused on the ball without becoming distracted.

"Hit!" when your racquet makes contact with the ball. This will force you to watch ball–racquet contact.

3. *Disregard future and past:* Play one point at a time. This means that between points you will have to concentrate only on the next point.

4. *Practice with appropriate distractions:* If you know you are going to play on panel walls, practice on panel courts. If you are playing in Houston in May, practice on hot and humid courts.

5. *Use cue words:* **Cue words** can remind you to trigger a certain response. For example, you may not be getting your racquet up and may say "Racquet up!" prior to ball contact. You may simply have a problem relaxing and need to say words like "relax" or "slow" to reduce anxiety.

6. Be nonjudgmental: Try not to assign a negative to your performance. If 50 percent of your drive serves are short, don't tell yourself you have a terrible drive serve. Simply tell yourself you have a high percentage of short serves and then change something (ball toss or contact point) to increase your percentage of good serves.

7. *Stick with your decisions:* In racquetball you must decide on shot selections very rapidly. Once you have selected a shot, stick with it so you can concentrate on the ball and the shot you are making. For example, once you have made the decision to "shoot down the line," don't change your mind in the middle of executing the shot.

▶ Ways to Improve Concentration

1. *Instructor behind student:* The instructor sets up the student from behind, with the student facing forward. As the ball leaves the front wall, the instructor yells out different shots. As the student becomes efficient at hitting these different shots, the instructor uses different-colored balls. Each color (two or three) indicates a different shot, and the instructor sets up the student but says nothing.

2. *Instructor behind and to the right of student:* The instructor hits the ball slowly at the student and tells what shot to hit. As practice continues the instructor hits the ball harder. As games get fast, players usually get tense, so this is a time for the student to practice relaxation techniques and concentrate on the ball. If you do this drill, set goals for each shot (for example, 10 nonreturnable pinches in a row). If you miss, you go back to zero. As you get close to 10, you will feel more tension and thus will need to use more concentration, which is great practice for game situations.

3. *Concentrating on the ball:* Place a ball in your hand and concentrate on the ball (the texture, color, label, etc.). Chart how long you can maintain concentration. Try to reach 5 minutes and then add distractions (TV, radio) and practice ignoring them.

4. *Pregame rehearsal:* Prior to a match rehearse situations that might come up and how you will respond. In this way you can precondition yourself to concentrate in difficult situations.

▶ **ASSIGNMENT—IMPROVING CONCENTRATION**

List five ways to improve your concentration while on the court.

1.

2.

3.

4.

5.

CONFIDENCE

The confidence inventory in this section will help you to evaluate your confidence about characteristics of yourself that are important to being successful in racquetball. As you probably know, athletes can have too little confidence, too much confidence, or just about the right degree of confidence.

Read each question carefully and think about your confidence with regard to each item as you competed over the last year. For each question indicate the percentage of the time you feel you have too little, too much, or just the right degree of confidence.

The sum of all three answers should be 100 percent, corresponding to 100 percent of the time you compete. For example, on a particular question you might answer 20 percent for "confidence too little," 70 percent for "confidence just right," and 10 percent for "confidence too much," adding up to 100 percent total. You may distribute the 100 percent in any way you think appropriate.

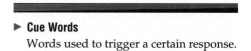

▶ **Cue Words**
Words used to trigger a certain response.

RACQUETBALL CONFIDENCE INVENTORY

With respect to your racquetball game, indicate the percentage of time you have

	Confidence Too Little	Confidence Just Right	Confidence Too Much

1. To make critical decisions in a game
2. To concentrate throughout a match
3. To perform under pressure
4. To return serves offensively
5. To return serves defensively
6. To control your emotions during a game
7. To come from behind and win
8. To improve your game
9. To accept criticism
10. To hit forehand kill shots
11. To hit backhand kill shots
12. To consistently serve well
13. To put forth the effort to succeed
14. To execute successful strategy
15. To anticipate your opponent's shots
16. To analyze opponent and develop pregame strategy
17. To be positive and optimistic

Reviewing your confidence inventory will demonstrate areas that need more work. For instance, if your inventory illustrates that you are not confident on about 80 percent of your backhand kills, then it would seem reasonable to spend more of your practice time working on this skill. With greater proficiency you will develop greater confidence and better mental toughness.

RELAXATION

The necessity for either **relaxation** or psyching up prior to and during a match varies from athlete to athlete. Some athletes perform better in a psyched-up condition, while others require a calm and relaxed demeanor to maximize performance.

Each athlete must determine his or her optimum flow state, that is, the mental state in which he or she maximizes performance. The flow state is the perfect mind and body state for performance. Ideally, each player wants to be physically warmed up, yet mentally calm and focused.

▶ Psych-Up Zone

The first zone in Figure 14-4, the **psych-up zone,** represents the time when the athlete is mentally and physically preparing for the match. The body and mind are not into their optimum energy zone yet.

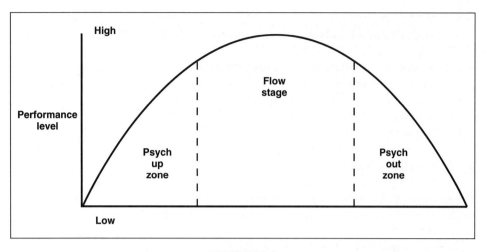

FIGURE 14-4

The psych-up state is the time prior to performance when the athlete is mentally and physically preparing for the match. Some athletes require a calming period while others require a time of excitement and getting "pumped up." Each athlete must determine which approach will help produce his or her best performance.

Here are a few ways to get psyched up for a match:

1. *Warm-up exercises:* Proper warm-up exercises (such as stretching and skipping) can warm up your body temperature by 1 degree Fahrenheit. This allows you to be loose, warmed up, and ready to perform your best.
2. *Breathing:* Deep breathing (for example, inhaling to the count of 4 and exhaling to the count of 4) can help relax you when stress and the pregame jitters hit.
3. *Mental activities:* You can listen to music, visualize your performance (discussed later in this chapter), repeat positive affirmations, review game strategies, and use any other mental exercises that help you prepare for the match.

▶ Flow State

As mentioned previously, **flow state** is the ideal mind and body state for performance. Each player strives to be physically warmed up at the start of the match but also mentally calm and focused. Here are some characteristics of the flow state:

▶ **Relaxation**
The ability to control one's emotions during a match.

▶ **Psych-Up Zone**
The time during which an athlete mentally and physically prepares for a match.

▶ **Flow State**
The ideal mind and body state (for competition).

- A feeling of high energy
- Mentally calm and focused
- Relaxed muscles and posture
- Freedom from anxiety and negative thoughts
- Confident, optimistic, alert
- A feeling of being "in complete control"
- Free of distractions
- Warmed up, sweating, and loose

▶ Psych-Out Zone

The third zone, the **psych-out zone,** occurs when an athlete starts to press or push too hard. In this zone, the athlete is overaroused, and there is usually a lack of confidence.

Here are some characteristics of the psych-out zone:

- Muscles are tight and contracted.
- Negative thoughts are prevalent.
- Timing, focus, and concentration are off.
- There is a lack of confidence.

When you start to get psyched out during a game, try the following:

1. *Do deep breathing:* Inhale through your nose to the count of 4 and exhale through your mouth to the count of 4. Relaxation will occur during exhalation.
2. *Refocus:* Concentrate on strings (or some other item), focus on the next rally, and "forget" previous rallies or crowd distractions.
3. *Cue words:* Use cue words to relax your body.
4. *Visualize:* Take a few seconds to visualize a positive image such as a perfect roll out.
5. *Take a time-out:* Take a break to hydrate, sit down, refocus, and relax.
6. *Diary review:* During a time-out, check your diary (which, of course, you always keep in your bag!). For example, if you are having difficulty with your forehand, check your diary forehand checklist (extension, follow-through, racquet prep, flat-stroke, etc.).
7. *Concentrate on the ball:* To refocus your attention, say "hit!" every time you contact the ball. This will help you concentrate on ball–racquet contact.

▶ Desire and Motivation

Before you develop any training program, you should ask yourself a question: "What price am I willing to pay to be the best that I can be?"

If your answer is, "I want to be the best, but because of my job, my family, school, and other obligations I may have to limit my training," then you may have to be more realistic and honest with yourself. If you truly want to "be the best" you will have to make sacrifices. There is a lot of truth in the statement "Winning is 10 percent inspiration and 90 percent perspiration."

The desire and motivation may be there at the beginning, but will you be able to maintain the intensity required to be the best you can be if you can't make the necessary sacrifices? After evaluating your commitments, you may want to reevaluate your goals, perhaps deciding to be the best you can be while working within the constraints of your current family and social commitments. Being realistic will reduce frustration and induce you to maintain the desire and motivation required to reach more realistic goals.

Desire and motivation come when you have a purpose (goal) in racquetball and then add passion for the game. There is no faster way to thwart passion than to be continually frustrated because of unrealistic objectives.

▶ Visualization

The art of visualization may be summarized thus: "What your mind can perceive and you truly believe, you can achieve." Here are some theories of **visualization** you should be familiar with when practicing visualization:

- Your mind doesn't know the difference between a vividly imagined picture and reality.
- An athlete's mind thinks in pictures before it thinks in words.
- The power of your imagination will determine the end result.
- Your muscles get a 30 percent neuromuscular contraction with each visualization.
- The deepest mental imprint comes when you incorporate as many senses (sight, sound, taste, smell, feel) into your visualization as possible.
- Partially moving your body in conjunction with your visualization increases the positive effects on the muscles.

The best time to practice visualization is the last thing at night and the first thing in the morning. At these times the brain is in a relaxed alpha state.

See yourself from the outside in, as if you were a spectator watching yourself. "Watch" yourself using perfect technique and form, positive and strong.

Next visualize yourself from the inside out, as through your own eyes. Visualize as if you were actually in the court, perfectly playing each ball. See the ball, the wall, your opponent, each stride, your perfect follow-through, and your movement after the hit.

Now stand up and use video dance or use partial movement to simulate mechanics.

In all visualizations, see yourself as being successful. See your actions and your posture as those of a winner.

▶ **Psych-Out Zone**
The time during which an athlete is over-aroused.

▶ **Visualization**
The art of perceiving in one's mind certain situations in great (lifelike) detail.

RACQUETBALL TRAINING DIARY

In order to build confidence, an athlete must keep a record of his or her training and competitive history. It is extremely important to be able to evaluate your performance, whether in competition or during training. The only way to really evaluate and compare the success of your training techniques is to chart or maintain records of performance and associated conditions. Say, for example, that you played well in a practice match on Monday but played terribly on Tuesday. Did you change your diet, your sleeping habits, your pregame rituals, your warm-up, your strategy? If you can compare conditions affecting performance, then you can make well-informed changes to improve performance. Some information to include in your training diary:

- Diet: percent fat, carbohydrates, protein; time of consumption
- Water: amount and frequency
- Sleep: quantity and quality
- Visualization practice: time of day, amount of time, quality
- Rituals: when, what kind, how you felt
- Training: when, amount, purpose, how you felt
- Attitude and Motivation: positive/negative, high/low
- Focus/concentration: distracted, in the moment
- Confidence: high/low
- Work/rest ratio: stress and recovery cycles
- Synergy: your overall daily performance

SAMPLE PERSONAL TRAINING DIARY

▶ Training Log

Practice/Game Session:

Place *Lynmar Racquet Club*

Time *10 a.m. to noon*

Date *2/12/98*

Warm-up:
1. 10–15 minutes of static stretching (right hamstring very tight!)
2. 5 minutes of skipping (hamstring still tight)

Techniques and Skill:
1. 15 minutes on drive serves—had trouble with FH—need to drop ball further
2. 15 minutes on ceiling balls—consistency good—good concentration
3. 15 minutes on BH pinches—need to concentrate on keeping elbow "in"

Strength:
No weights today (no time)

Physical:

1. 20 minutes of speed training—good technique, but got tired—maintained rate at 70% throughout

Overall:

Good workout—felt good—fatigued during physical but may be because of rough day before

RACQUETBALL COMPETITIVE DIARY

Competitive diaries are somewhat similar to training diaries, but instead of logging training information you record your competitive performance, as well as your opponent's performance. Some information to include in your competitive diaries:

Opponent:

1. Name of opponent, date of match, division of play, time of match, number of match in the day (second round, etc.)
2. Opponent's strengths and weaknesses
3. Strategies of opponent that worked and those that didn't
4. Comments on what to change when facing this opponent in the future

Your game:

1. Diet, mood, confidence, energy level at time of game
2. Shots that worked and shots that didn't
3. Your strengths and weaknesses
4. Distractions, focus
5. Overall feelings

When practicing, it is a good idea to write down areas in which you have problems and, below the problem area, list solutions. Then, during a match, it is easy to take a time-out and quickly review your notes. Try to keep each section short so you don't get confused and concentrate only on a few points. For example:

Problem: skipping backhand

Solution:

- hitting ball too close—extend swing
- concentrate on racquet prep
- level out swing—hit cross-court first few shots in order to level out swing

SUMMARY

- Athletes must train as hard mentally as they do physically if they want to achieve elite status.
- Training diaries are important tools to use in order to determine what works and what doesn't for a particular athlete.

DRILLS TO IMPROVE YOUR GAME

After reading this chapter, you should be able to do the following:

- Illustrate various drills that will assist in improving skills.
- Outline certain errors and how to correct them.

KEY TERM

While reading this chapter, you will become familiar with the following term:

► Target Serving

Drills are designed to help the athlete work on technique, improve consistency and efficiency, and develop confidence. It is important to make sure your technique is correct when drilling. To practice with improper technique only reinforces bad habits, which have a tendency to reappear during competition. A good way to verify good technique is to videotape your drilling sessions and review the video-tape after drilling.

Here are some basics about drilling:

1. Drills are practice exercises designed to increase skill proficiency, increase confidence, and develop shots.
2. Limit your focus. Different drills focus on different skills, so be specific.
3. Set goals for each drill—for example, 25 ceiling balls that do not result in an offensive opportunity.
4. Drill under both practice and game conditions.
5. Increase your goals and expectations as your skills increase.
6. Each drill should be preceded by visualization of the perfect shot.
7. It's the quality of drilling that is important, not the quantity.
8. Write down your goals, your drills, and your results.
9. Each drill should be practiced first for accuracy, second for power.
10. Perfection/measurement of drills are judged by the accomplishment of your goals—for example, if your goal is to hit 10 perfect kills and you only hit 6 you have not accomplished your goal or perfection of the drill.

SERVICE DRILLS

Remember that 27 percent of all rallies in racquetball are won on the serve. Although the only time you can score is when you are serving, few players spend any time practicing their serves. This is a mistake you should avoid. The following drills will help improve your accuracy and consistency.

TARGET SERVING—FRONT WALL

Hit what you believe is a good drive serve. Have someone mark where the ball hit the front wall. After analyzing the serve (was it short, long, too high, bad angle, etc.), keep changing the location of the front-wall marker until you hit a *perfect serve*. Now attempt to hit 10 good serves by aiming at the marker.

TARGET SERVING—DIFFERENT LOCATIONS

Place your racquetball bag in the back corner where you want your lob serve to land. You can practice using different locations depending on your objectives (for example, in deep corner where ball lands on second bounce). Place tape on the side wall where you want your high lob off the side wall to hit. Move the tape each time you hit until your lob serve is perfected. (It

▶ **Target Serving**
Selecting targets (on the wall, floor, etc.) which result in perfect serves.

should be high and deep enough to make cutoff difficult and deep enough so the second bounce doesn't come off the back wall.)

ONE LOCATION VARIATION

Select a position in the service box (near the center) where you like to serve from. Practice hitting at least four different serves from the same service box location. Serve to both sides. Attempt to increase percentages of good serves for each type of serve.

ONE SERVE—SECOND-SERVE OFFENSIVE

Practice one kind of serve attempting to get close to 100 percent first-serve accuracy. After you have achieved your designated goal, change to a different kind of serve. Practice offensive serves (drives, jams) as second-serve weapons. Develop a high consistency percentage. This will also help with your first serve in game situations.

SIMULATED GAMES (WITH A PARTNER)

There are a variety of ways to practice games, such as using only one serve, using only drive serves for second serve, giving the server two points for an ace, or having the server serve five times before switching with the opponent. You can even create your own game. Another good simulation game is when the receiver gets points if he or she wins the rally but doesn't have to be the server. To practice various serving techniques, you can play that the server must use a different serve from the same location every time.

SERVICE RETURN DRILLS

Since 22 percent of all rallies are won on the service return and a weak return obviously gives the opponent an immediate advantage, it is important to spend time practicing service return.

OFFENSIVE RETURNS

Be aggressive and offensive with all returns. Practice one type of offensive shot at a time until consistency is developed. Every time a return ends up in a set up or an offensive opportunity is available, the server gets a point.

5-POINT GAMES

For this practice game variation, the server works on one serve and the opponent on an aggressive return of the serve. There are no rallies after the receiver hits the ball. Good returns get one point, and a good serve with weak return gives the server one point. Change server after 5 points. After each player serves, change the serve and type of return.

BACKWALL DRILLS

SIMULATION—NO RACQUET—ONE BOUNCE

This no-racquet drill will help your timing and footwork. Stand facing the side wall with your racquet hand facing the back wall. Throw the ball with your opposite hand against the back wall. Shuffle-step sideways, and after the ball bounces once on the floor, catch the ball. Attempt to consistently catch the ball with your racquet hand near your front foot. After you accomplish this goal, switch to backhand.

SIMULATION—NO RACQUET—NO BOUNCE

This drill is similar to the previous one but you bounce the ball on the floor before it hits the back wall and then catch the ball in the air as it comes off the back wall. Use the same shuffle step with bent knees.

SIMULATION—WITH RACQUET

Similar to the previous drill but the ball goes front wall, back wall, bounces, and then you make contact. Variations may be ceiling ball, bounces, back wall, and then you make contact; or front wall, bounces, back wall, and then you make contact.

BACK WALL WITH PARTNER

In this drill your partner sets you up off the back wall. Each player gets five setups and you play out each point after a setup. The first player to get 15 points wins. If you win the rally on the first shot off the back wall you get 2 points.

PASSING SHOTS DRILLS

Passing shots work as both defensive and offensive shots. They allow you to move your opponent out of center court, thus putting you in a better position. They also are very high percentage shots since there is so much room for error. Even if the pass shot is not perfect, it normally will cause your opponent to run to deep court and turn completely around, and thus force a difficult shot in which you have perfect court position.

WIDE-ANGLE PASS

Wide-angle passes (Figure 15-1) are designed to hit the side wall just behind the 5-foot receiving line. Your opponent's defensive position is normally in this area, and by hitting the side wall parallel to where he or she is located you are forcing your opponent to go the maximum distance in order to retrieve the ball. It is almost impossible to retrieve the ball before it hits the side wall. If it is retrieved off the side wall, the ball usually jams your opponent or forces a weak defensive return. Practice first by simply dropping the ball and hitting the wide-angle shot. You may want to place a target on the floor directly below where you are aiming. Also, once you determine the correct angle, place a target on the front wall to reinforce your front-wall location.

After you accomplish your objectives with drop and hit, set yourself up off the front wall and again repeat the drill, hitting the correct angle. This drill has a number of variations—set up off the ceiling ball, off the back wall, off the side-wall angle, and so on. Change the drill but remember to always concentrate on your front-wall target, your side-wall target, and getting the proper angle.

CROSS-COURT PASS

The cross-court pass (Figure 15-2) is hit at an angle so that the ball travels to the opposite corner. The shot is normally hit when your opponent is out of position, thus forcing him or her to retreat to deep court in order to receive the ball.

Similar to the approach described previously for practicing the wide-angle pass, place your targets in the appropriate areas (front wall, deep corner) and practice first with a drop and hit, then with a front-wall setup, and then with variations that require you to use different kinds of footwork. Remember to use this shot only when your opponent is out of position or when he or she has a very weak side. If your opponent is properly positioned, the cross-court pass will normally be retrieved after only one step and a swing, and thus you may want to use another shot in this situation.

CEILING-BALL DRILLS

CONTINUAL HITS—SOLO

Select a number and attempt to hit that many consecutive good ceiling balls from your forehand side. After your goal is accomplished, switch to the backhand. Next, hit a preselected number of ceiling balls alternating forehand and backhand.

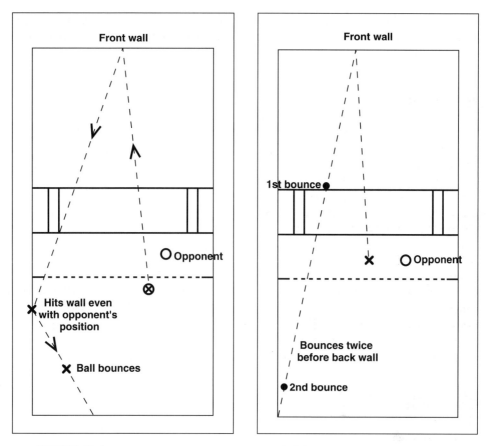

FIGURE 15-1 Wide-angle pass.   **FIGURE 15-2** Cross-court pass.

Once your goal is accomplished, hit a forehand ceiling ball from the forehand side and return with a cross-court forehand ceiling ball. Move to the backhand side, return with a down-the-line backhand ceiling ball, return with a cross-court backhand ceiling ball, and then move to forehand side and repeat the drill. This drill forces you to move and hit both forehand and backhand ceiling balls.

CONTINUAL HITS—PARTNER

Alternate with your partner hitting cross-court ceiling balls. After your goals are accomplished, switch sides. To include the conditioning aspect, hit ceiling balls to your partner but include a run to the 5-foot line and back between each ceiling ball.

OVERHEAD SLAM DRILL

Have your partner serve high lobs and Z-lobs to your forehand. Return with overhead slams first down-the-line. Concentrate on moving your opponent out of the service box, backward. If your opponent gets to the ball, he or she should be forced to hit the ball at waist level or above. Next hit cross-court passes (both wide-angle and regular). Speed on overhead slams is critical. If hit too hard, an overhead slam will rebound off the back wall, and if hit too easy, it will turn into an easy setup for your opponent.

SHORT-HOP SERVES DRILLS

This is one of the most difficult shots to execute in racquetball. Common errors when executing this shot are: (1) approaching the ball too straight on, (2) dropping the back shoulder, (3) not rotating the shoulders on contact, and (4) hitting the ball too close to body. The remainder of the chapter outlines ways to correct these errors.

BALL APPROACH

Approach the ball at an angle. This will force you to rotate and make contact with your feet perpendicular to the side wall. If you approach the ball too straight on, you tend to have your feet facing forward, thus blocking any body rotation.

DROPPING BACK SHOULDER

Many players have a tendency to drop their back shoulder, thus causing an upward pendulum motion swing. Concentrate on bending your knees and dipping your front shoulder into the ball.

NO BODY ROTATION

Many players simply swing using only their arm due to either poor footwork or improper body positioning. When approaching the ball, concentrate on making sure your shoulders are rotated. A good way to check this is to have the printing on the back of your shirt (if there is any) facing the server. This will force your shoulders to rotate and your hips to be in proper alignment for ball contact.

HITTING THE BALL TOO CLOSE TO THE BODY

This is a common error for many players, not only on short hops but also during the rallies. Hitting the ball too close to your body will often cause your racquet head to drop and restrict both shoulder and hip rotation.

SUMMARY

- To improve skills and consistency, the racquetball player must practice a series of drills.
- Drilling should be performed with specific goals and guidelines in mind.

Appendix A

PEAK TRAINING

As a relatively young sport, dominated by recreational and weekend athletes, racquetball has given little attention to developing proper training techniques. To do so requires comparison to similar sports, followed by research to substantiate the techniques.

That research has been conducted at the U.S. Olympic Training Center under the direction of Dr. Alan Salmoni of Laurentian University for the past 10 years. This has become the most comprehensive study performed on racquetball athletes to date, and the data gathered provides a basis for developing a complete training schedule.

The following schedules and information may be applied to any level of racquetball athlete. The more dedicated and serious player will, of course, spend more time on each level of training, while the weekend recreational player may only adopt a small portion of the complete program.

Research indicates that an athlete *can only hold a peak performance level for a maximum of 2 or 3 weeks,* making it important for you to schedule your training to peak for the most important competitions. Knowing this, you can take the time to schedule your entire season to pinpoint tournaments and determine which events will be "peak" tournaments for you. When you plan in this way, you'll see that you can only "peak" two or three times per year.

DEVELOPING A COMPLETE TRAINING SCHEDULE

All serious athletes plan their play and play their plan. Once you determine your peak events and your training schedule, it is important that you follow your plan. Periodic adjustments may be made to include new tournaments or to attend to personal schedules, but you should put every effort into maintaining your overall plan.

The training schedule developed for racquetball is divided into four phases:
1. Introductory or base phase
2. Strength phase
3. Power phase
4. Maintenance phase

A COMPLETE TRAINING SCHEDULE

In this sample schedule we break the racquetball season into two competitive periods.

The first competitive period would begin June 1 and end December 31. The second period would begin January 1 and end May 31.

The reason for dividing the season into two sections is to eliminate training boredom and to separate summer and winter periods in which many players concentrate on doubles and singles, respectively.

Of course you may want to develop only one training schedule for the entire season, in which case you would simply make each phase longer.

Introductory Phase I—Off-Season

Time of season
Dividing year into two competitive seasons
    June 1–July 15   1st off-season
    January 1–February 1   2nd off-season
Purpose—To take a mental break from competition and perhaps racquetball in general. To develop or maintain general conditioning.
Racquetball skills—Little time spent on racquetball skills; play just to maintain timing and for fun!
Areas of concentration—Aerobic conditioning, flexibility, mental skills.

Phase II Preseason I—Strength

Time of season
    July 15–September 1
    February 1–March 1
Purpose—To train muscles involved in racquetball. To attain the strength needed for racquetball.
Racquetball skills—some time spent on skills and playing; continuation of mental skills training.
Areas of concentration—Aerobic maintenance, speed training, flexibility, mental skills. Isolation of wrist, arms, shoulders, and lower body for strength development.

Phase III Preseason II—Power

Time of season
    September 1—October 15
    March 1—April 1
Purpose—To work on the development of power in order to maximize ball velocity and body movement.
Racquetball skills—Begin to spend more time on court and to work on skills.
Areas of concentration—Multiple joint exercises focusing on explosive power (legs, arms, wrists, shoulders). Step work, racquetball skills, mental skills.

Phase IV—In-Season Maintenance

Time of season
    October 15—December 20
    April 1—May 31
Purpose—To peak for important competition(s). To maintain conditioning effects developed in first three phases.
Racquetball skills—Specifically working on skills required for competition. Reviewing and analyzing game plans and strategies.
Areas of concentration—Racquetball and mental skills, speed work.

Appendix B

RACQUETBALL EYEGUARDS: Abbreviated List
(Updated: May 28, 1998)
According to the manufacturer, the following models of protective eyewear meet ASTM or CSA impact standards for racquetball, as specified in USRA rule 2.5(a).

RULE 2.5 APPAREL

(a) Lensed eyewear designed for racquetball, which meets or exceeds ASTM F803 or Canadian (CSA) impact standards, is required apparel. This rule applies to all persons, including those who must wear corrective lenses. The eyewear must be worn as designed and at all times. A player who fails to wear proper eyewear will be assessed a technical foul and a timeout to obtain proper eyewear. A second infraction in the same match will result in immediate forfeiture of the match. (See Rule 4.18(a)(9).

RULE 4.18 TECHNICAL FOULS AND WARNINGS (ABBREVIATED)

(a) Technical Fouls. The referee is empowered to deduct one point from a player's or team's score when, in the referee's sole judgment, the player is being overtly and deliberately abusive. If the player or team against whom the technical foul was assessed does not resume play immediately, the referee is empowered to forfeit the match in favor of the opponent. Some examples of actions which may result in technical fouls are: 9. Failure to wear lensed eyewear designed for racquet sports is an automatic technical foul on the first infraction and a mandatory timeout will be charged against the offending player to acquire the proper eyewear. A second infraction by that player during the match will result in automatic forfeiture of the match.

PLEASE NOTE: The ASTM standard cited in rule 2.5 addresses the impact resistance of the tested eyeguards **as a unit.** This means that the lens and frame **combination** meets the cited safety standard. For those who must wear corrective lenses, it is **not** acceptable to merely have impact resistant lens material placed in everyday, fashion eyeglass frames. Please use the following list (or the expanded version with prices and vendor information) to select a suitable model for your protection.

Manufacturer	Models
BLACK KNIGHT	Action Eyes; Action Eyes (small); Black Knight Sight Guard; Turbo; Vista.
EAGLE EYEWEAR, INC.	Rep 1—small and large; Rep 2.
EKTELON	Mirage; Olympus; Odyssey; Quantum; Scopa; Spector.
ITECH SPORT PRODUCTS/RBE INC.	Itech Reflex; Itech Sonic; Itech Sonic II; Itech Pro Sonic; Itech Super Sonic.
KLEERSHOT, INC.	Kleershot.
LEADER	Albany; Brittany; Champion; Dallas; Maxum; New Yorker; Optiview; Ultima; Vizion 2.
LIBERTY OPTICAL	All Pro Rec Specs/large (59-17); All Pro Rec Specs/small [54-15]; Demon [54]; Demon [51]; Demon [48]; Junior Small Rec Spec [45-15]; Mantis [59]; Mantis [57]; Raptor [59]; Raptor [56]; Rec Specs for Kids [45-15/40-15]; Rec Specs/X-Large [51-17]; Rec Specs/small [45-15]; Sport-Lok [57-14]; Sport-Lok [60-14]; Sport Goggle II [57-20]; Wrap I by Rec Specs [59-17/54-17]; Wrap I by Rec Specs [45-15/42-15]; Wrap II by Rec Specs [57-20].
NORTH ATLANTIC SERVICES, INC.	Thor [small/medium/large].
PROKENNEX	Pro Kleer.
RAD/ADVANCE CORP.	Feather JR 5020J; Neon 3284; Turbo AL0004; Turbo LX0004.
REM OPTICAL CO./CONVERSE SPORTS EYEGEAR	M.V.P.; Sport Goggle 1; Sport Goggle 2; Sport Goggle 3; Switch Hitter.
R.P.M. DISTRIBUTORS	Safetylite.
SPALDING	Delray [#1085]; Pasadena [#1090]; San Luis [#1200]; San Diego [#1300]; San Mateo [#1600]; Sacramento [#2000].

UNIQUE SPORTS PRODUCTS INC.   Fashion Racket Specs; Pro View; RX Specs; Super Specs; Youth Super Specs.

WILSON RACQUETBALL   Aero Spec; Court Hawk; Focus; Omni; Phantom; Sitex; Tempo; Vista.

Racquetball Eyeguards
[Updated: May 28, 1998]
According to the manufacturer, the following models of protective eyewear meet ASTM or CSA impact standards for racquetball, as specified in USRA rule 2.5(a).

Keys to special features:
  (RX) = Accepts prescription or plano lens
  (A) = May be worn by youngsters through adults
  (C) = Designed for head size of children
  (O) = Designed to wear over RX eyewear

COMPANY & EYEWEAR DESCRIPTION

BLACK KNIGHT
5355 SIERRA ROAD—SAN JOSE, CA 95132
408/923-7777; 408/923-7794 (fax)
  Action Eyes (RX) (A)
  Action Eyes (small) (RX)(C)
  Black Knight Sight Guard (A)
  Turbo [Model 7000] (A)
  Vista [Model 8000] (A)

EAGLE EYEWEAR, INC.
P.O. BOX 486 – WHITEHOUSE, NJ 08888
UPS: 89 MAIN STREET, LEBANON, NJ 08833
908/236-9300; 908/236-9301 (fax)
  Rep 1-small and large (RX)(A)(C)
  Rep 2 (RX)(A)

EKTELON
1 SPORTSYSTEM PLAZA (P.O. BOX 151)
BORDENTOWN, NJ 08505
609/293-5800; 609/291-5794 (fax); 800/283-6647
  Mirage (A)
  Olympus (A)
  Odyssey (A)
  Quantum (A)
  Scopa (A)
  Spector (A)

ITECH SPORT PRODUCTS / RBE INC.
ROUTE 104A ARROWHEAD INDUSTRIAL PARK
FAIRFAX, VERMONT 05454
800/247-4639; 800/ 743-6313 (fax); 514/421-0224
  Itech Reflex (A)
  Itech Sonic (A)
  Itech Sonic II (A)
  Itech Pro Sonic (A)
  Itech Super Sonic (A)

KLEERSHOT, INC.
15917 HARMONY WAY – APPLE VALLEY, MN 55124
612/432-9732; 612/432-9732 (fax)
  Kleershot (RX)(A)(C)

LEADER
43 NORTH COUNTRY SHOPPING CENTER
PLATTSBURGH, NY 12901-7209
800/847-2001; 518/562-1819
  Albany (A)
  Brittany (A)
  Champion (O)
  Dallas (A)
  Maxum (A)
  New Yorker (A)
  Optiview (A)
  Ultima (A)
  Vizion 2 (O)

LIBERTY OPTICAL
380 VERONA AVENUE – NEWARK, NJ 07104
201/484-4100; 201/484-3446 (fax); 800/444-5010
  All Pro Rec Specs/large [59-17] (RX)(A)
  All Pro Rec Specs/small [54-15] (RX)(A)
  Demon [54] (RX)(A)
  Demon [51] (RX)(A)
  Demon [48] (RX)(C)
  Junior Small Rec Spec [45-15](RX)(C)
  Mantis [59] (RX)(A)
  Mantis [57] (RX)(C)
  Raptor [59] (RX)(A)
  Raptor [56] (RX)(A)
  Rec Specs for Kids [45-15/40-15] (RX)(C)
  Rec Specs/X-Large [51-17] (RX)(A)
  Rec Specs/small [45-15] (RX)(C)
  Sport-Lok [57-14] (RX)(A)
  Sport-Lok [60-14] (RX)(A)

Sport Goggle II [57-20] (RX)(A)
Wrap I by Rec Specs [59-17/54-17] (RX)(A)
Wrap I by Rec Specs [45-15/42-15] (RX)(C)
Wrap II by Rec Specs [57-20] (RX)(A)

NORTH ATLANTIC SERVICES, INC.
39 ANGUS LANE—GREENWICH, CT 06831
800/223-5127; 800/626-6933 (fax)
Thor [small/medium/large] (RX)(A)(C)

PROKENNEX
9606 KEARNY VILLA ROAD—SAN DIEGO, CA 92126
800/854-1908; 619/566-3686 (fax)
Pro Kleer (RX)(AC)

RAD by ADVANCE CORPORATION
249 EAST 5TH STREET—LOS ANGELES, CA 90013
213/892-1062; 312/892-1049 (fax)
Feather JR 5020J
Neon 3284
Turbo AL0004
Turbo LX0004

REM OPTICAL CO. / CONVERSE SPORTS EYEGEAR
9301 LAUREL CANYON BLVD.—ARLETA, CA 91331
800/423-3023; 818/504-3966 (fax)
M.V.P. (A)
Sport Goggle 1 (RX)(A)
Sport Goggle 2 (RX)(A)
Sport Goggle 3 (RX)(A)
Switch Hitter (RX)(A)

R.P.M. DISTRIBUTORS
1107 RIVARA ROAD—STOCKTON, CA 95207
209/957-3542; 209/957-3542 Ext 51 (fax); 800/484-9851 ext. 3339
Safetylite (RX)(A)

SPALDING
FLAIR MARKETING CORPORATION
375 SYLVAN AVENUE—ENGLEWOOD CLIFFS, NJ 07632
201/894-8050; 201/894-5964; 201/894-8041 (fax)
Delray [#1085] (RX)(A)
Pasadena [#1090] (A)
San Luis [#1200] (RX)(A,C)
San Diego [#1300] (A)(C)
San Mateo [#1600] (RX)(A)
Sacramento [#2000] (RX)(A)

UNIQUE SPORTS PRODUCTS INC.
840 MCFARLAND ROAD—ALPHARETTA, GA 30004
770/442-1977; 770/475-2065 (fax); 800/554-3707
  Fashion Racket Specs (RX)(A)
  Great Specs (A)
  Pro View (A)
  RX Specs (RX)(A)
  Super Specs (A)
  Youth Super Specs

WILSON RACQUETBALL
7670 TRADE STREET, SUITE B—SAN DIEGO, CA 92121
619/586-0300; 619/586-0896 (fax)
  Aero Spec
  Court Hawk
  Omni (A)
  Vista (A)
  Sitex
  Tempo (RX)(A)
  Phantom (A)
  Focus (A)

Appendix C

GUIDEBOOKS AND BROCHURES

Tournament Director's Guidebook
Officiating Racquetball
Collegiate Guidebook
High School Manual
Junior Manual
Junior Development Package (includes Junior Manual)
Weight Resistance Training for Racquetball
Nutrition Brochure
Mental Skills Training Brochure

INSTRUCTIONAL TAPES

Learn your Lessons I: A Fundamental Approach to the Basics with Fran Davis &
    Stu Hastings (24 minutes)
Learn your Lessons II: Drills with Dave George & Connie Martin (25 minutes)
Learn your Lessons III: Advanced Racquetball with Diana McNab, Scott Phelps &
    Jim Winterton (27 minutes, w/audiotape & training manual)

Appendix D

United States Racquetball Association (USRA)
U.S. Olympic Committee recognized
National Governing Body
1685 West Uintah
Colorado Springs, CO 80904-2921
Tel: 719/635-5396
Fax: 719/635-0685

International Health & Racquet Sports Association [IHRSA]
253 Summer Street
Boston, MA 02110
Tel: 800/228-IRSA

International Racquetball Federation
International Olympic Committee
recognized International Federation
1685 West Uintah
Colorado Springs, CO 80904-2921
Tel: 719/635-5396
Fax: 719/635-0685

Women's International Racquetball Tour (WIRT)
International Racquetball Tour [IRT]
Women's and Men's Professional Associations
13735 Regency Court
Lake Oswego, OR 97035
Tel: 403/639-3410

State Racquetball Associations
USRA recognized State Governing Bodies—Complete listing available on request
from USRA

American Professional Racquetball Association [AMPRO]
Professional Instructors, Coaches & Program Directors
1685 West Uintah
Colorado Springs, CO 80904-2921
Tel: 719/635-5396
Fax: 719/635-0685

153

Appendix E

THE GAME

RULE 1.1 TYPES OF GAMES

Racquetball is played by two or four players. When played by two, it is called singles and when played by four, doubles. A non-tournament variation of the game that is played by three players is called cutthroat.

RULE 1.2 DESCRIPTION

Racquetball is a competitive game in which a strung racquet is used to serve and return the ball.

RULE 1.3 OBJECTIVE

The objective is to win each rally by serving or returning the ball so the opponent is unable to keep the ball in play. A rally is over when a player (or team in doubles) is unable to hit the ball before it touches the floor twice, is unable to return the ball in such a manner that it touches the front wall before it touches the floor, or when a hinder is called.

RULE 1.4 POINTS AND OUTS

Points are scored only by the serving side when it serves an irretrievable serve (an ace) or wins a rally. Losing the serve is called a sideout in singles. In doubles, when the first server loses the serve it is called a handout and when the second server loses the serve it is a sideout.

RULE 1.5 MATCH, GAME, TIEBREAKER

A match is won by the first side winning two games. The first two games of a match are played to 15 points. If each side wins one game, a tiebreaker game is played to 11 points.

COURTS AND EQUIPMENT

RULE 2.1 COURT SPECIFICATIONS

The specifications for the standard four-wall racquetball court are:

I. Dimensions. The dimensions shall be 20 feet wide, 40 feet long and 20 feet high, with a back wall at least 12 feet high. All surfaces shall be in play, with the exception of any gallery opening, surfaces designated as out-of-play for a valid reason (such as being of a very different material or not in alignment with the backwall), and designated court hinders.

II. Markings. Racquetball courts shall be marked with lines 1½ inches wide as follows:
   A. Short Line. The back edge of the short line is midway between, and is parallel with, the front and back walls.
   B. Service Line. The front edge of the service line is parallel with, and five feet in front of, the back edge of the short line.
   C. Service Zone. The service zone is the 5' × 20' area bounded by the bottom edges of the side walls and by the outer edges of the short line and the service line.
   D. Service Boxes. The service boxes are located at each end of the service zone and are designated by lines parallel with the side walls. The edge of the line nearest to the center of the court shall be 18 inches from the nearest side wall.
   E. Drive Serve Lines. The drive serve lines, which form the drive serve zone, are parallel with the side wall and are within the service zone. The edge of the line nearest to the center of the court shall be three feet from the nearest side wall.
   F. Receiving Line. The receiving line is a broken line parallel to the short line. The back edge of the receiving line is five feet from the back edge of the short line. The receiving line begins with a line 21 inches long that extends from each side wall. These lines are connected by an alternate series of six-inch spaces and six-inch lines. This will result in a line composed of 17 six-inch spaces, 16 six-inch lines, and two 21-inch lines.
   G. Safety Zone. The safety zone is the 5' × 20' area bounded by the bottom edges of the side walls and by the back edges of the short line and the receiving line. The zone is observed only during the serve. See Rules 3.10(IX) and 3.11(A).

RULE 2.2 BALL SPECIFICATIONS

I. The standard racquetball shall be 2¼ inches in diameter; weigh approximately 1.4 ounces; have a hardness of 55–60 inches durometer; and bounce 68–72 inches from a 100-inch drop at a temperature of 70–74 degrees Fahrenheit.

II. Only a ball having the endorsement or approval of the USRA may be used in a USRA sanctioned tournament.

RULE 2.3 BALL SELECTION

I. A ball shall be selected by the referee for use in each match. During the match the referee may, based on personal discretion or at the request of a player or team, replace the ball. Balls that are not round or which bounce erratically shall not be used.

II. If possible, the referee and players should agree to an alternate ball, so that in the event of breakage, the second ball can be put into play immediately.

RULE 2.4 RACQUET SPECIFICATIONS

I. The racquet, including bumper guard and all solid parts of the handle, may not exceed 22 inches in length.

II. The racquet frame may be any material judged to be safe.

III. The racquet frame must include a cord that must be securely attached to the player's wrist.

IV. The string of the racquet must be gut, monofilament, nylon, graphite, plastic, metal, or a combination thereof, and must not mark or deface the ball.

V. Using an illegal racquet will result in forfeiture of the game in progress or, if discovered between games, forfeiture of the preceding game.

RULE 2.5 APPAREL

I. All players must wear lensed eyewear that has been warranted by its manufacturer or distributor as (i) designed for use in racquetball and (ii) meeting or exceeding either the full ASTM F803 standard or Canadian (CSA) impact standard. This rule applies to all persons, including those who wear corrective lenses. The eyewear must be unaltered and worn as designed at all times. A player who fails to wear proper eyewear will be assessed a technical foul and a timeout to obtain proper eyewear. A second infraction in the same match will result in immediate forfeiture of the match.

The USRA maintains a complete list of all eyewear so warranted by their manufacturers, and distributes the current list to the directors of every sanctioned event. In addition the list is published on the Internet at http://www.usra.org/ PUB&REF/eyeguard.htm, and may appear periodically in RACQUETBALL. A printed list is also made available upon request from the USRA's National Office [719/635-5396].

Eyewear NOT on the then-current list CANNOT be used in sanctioned events. An eyewear list with a date more than 60 days past the first day of the tournament will be deemed invalid for the purpose of determining compliance with this eyewear rule.

II. Clothing and Shoes. The clothing may be of any color; however, a player may be required to change wet, extremely loose fitting, or otherwise distracting garments. Insignias and writing on the clothing must be considered to be in good taste by the tournament director. Shoes must have soles which do not mark or damage the floor.

III. Equipment Requirements During Warm-up. Proper eyeguards [see 2.5(I)] must be worn and wrist cords must be used during any on-court warm-up period. The referee should give a technical warning to any person who fails to comply and assess a technical foul if that player continues to not comply after receiving such a warning.

PLAY REGULATIONS

RULE 3.1 SERVE

The server will have two opportunities to put the ball into play. The player or team winning the coin toss has the option to either serve or receive at the start of the first game. The second game will begin in reverse order of the first game. The player or team scoring the highest total of points in games 1 and 2 will have the option to serve or receive first at the start of the tiebreaker. In the event that both players or teams score an equal number of points in the first two games, another coin toss will take place and the winner of the toss will have the option to serve or receive.

RULE 3.2 START

The server may not start the service motion until the referee has called the score or "second serve." The serve is started from any place within the service zone. (Certain drive serves are an exception. See Rule 3.6.) Neither the ball nor any part of either foot may extend beyond either line of the service zone when initiating the service motion. Stepping on, but not beyond, the lines is permitted. However, when completing the service motion, the server may step beyond the service (front) line provided that some part of both feet remain on or inside the line until the served ball passes the short line. The server may not step beyond the short line until the ball passes the short line. See Rule 3.9(A) and 3.10(IX) for penalties for violations.

RULE 3.3 MANNER

After taking a set position inside the service zone, a player may begin the service motion—any continuous movement which results in the ball being served. Once the service motion begins, the ball must be bounced on the floor in the zone and be struck by the racquet before it bounces a second time. After being struck, the ball must hit the front wall first and on the rebound hit the floor beyond the back edge of the short line, either with or without touching one of the side walls.

RULE 3.4 READINESS

The service motion shall not begin until the referee has called the score or the second serve and the server has visually checked the receiver. The referee shall call the score as both server and receiver prepare to return to their respective positions, shortly after the previous rally has ended.

RULE 3.5 DELAYS

Except as noted in Rule 3.5 (II), the referee may call a technical foul for delays exceeding 10 seconds.

I.   The 10 second rule applies to the server and receiver simultaneously. Collectively, they are allowed up to 10 seconds after the score is called to serve or be ready to receive. It is the server's responsibility to look and be certain the receiver is ready. If a receiver is not ready, they must signal by raising the racquet above the head or completely turning the back to the server. (These are the only two acceptable signals.)

II. Serving while the receiving player/team is signaling not ready is a fault serve.

III. After the score is called, if the server looks at the receiver and the receiver is not signaling not ready, the server may then serve. If the receiver attempts to signal not ready after that point, the signal shall not be acknowledged and the serve becomes legal.

RULE 3.6 DRIVE SERVICE ZONES

The drive serve lines will be 3 feet from each side wall in the service zone. Viewed one at a time, the drive serve line divides the service area into a 3-foot and a 17-foot section that apply only to drive serves. The player may drive serve between the body and the side wall nearest to where the service motion began only if the player starts and remains outside of the 3-foot drive service zone. In the event that the service motion begins in one 3-foot drive service zone and continues into the other 3-foot drive serve zone, the player may not hit a drive serve at all.

I.   The drive serve zones are not observed for cross-court drive serves, the hard-Z, soft-Z, lob or half-lob serves.

II. The racquet may not break the plane of the 17-foot zone while making contact with the ball.

III. The drive serve line is not part of the 17-foot zone. Dropping the ball on the line or standing on the line while serving to the same side is an infraction.

RULE 3.7 DEFECTIVE SERVES

Defective serves are of three types resulting in penalties as follows:

I. Dead-Ball Serve. A dead-ball serve results in no penalty and the server is given another serve (without canceling a prior fault serve).

II. Fault Serve. Two fault serves result in an out (either a sideout or a handout).

III. Out Serve. An out serve results in an out (either a sideout or a handout).

RULE 3.8 DEAD-BALL SERVES

Dead-ball serves do not cancel any previous fault serve. The following are dead-ball serves:

I. Court Hinders. A serve that takes an irregular bounce because it hit a wet spot or an irregular surface on the court is a dead-ball serve. Also, any serve that hits any surface designated by local rules as an obstruction rather than being out-of-play.

II. Broken Ball. If the ball is determined to have broken on the serve, a new ball shall be substituted and the serve shall be replayed, not canceling any prior fault serve.

RULE 3.9 FAULT SERVES

The following serves are faults and any two in succession result in an out:

I. Foot Faults. A foot fault results when:
   A. The server does not begin the service motion with both feet in the service zone.
   B. The server steps completely over the service line (no part of the foot on or inside the service zone) before the served ball crosses the short line.

II. Short Service. A short serve is any served ball that first hits the front wall and, on the rebound, hits the floor on or in front of the short line either with or without touching a side wall.

III. Three Wall Serve. A three-wall serve is any served ball that first hits the front wall and, on the rebound, strikes both side walls before touching the floor.

IV. Ceiling Serve. A ceiling serve is any served ball that first hits the front wall and then touches the ceiling (with or without touching a side wall).

V. Long Serve. A long serve is a served ball that first hits the front wall and rebounds to the back wall before touching the floor (with or without touching a side wall).

VI Bouncing Ball Outside Service Zone. Bouncing the ball outside the service zone as a part of the service motion is a fault serve.

VII. Illegal Drive Serve. A drive serve in which the player fails to observe the 17-foot drive service zone outlined in Rule 3.6.

VIII. Screen Serve. A served ball that first hits the front wall and on the rebound passes so closely to the server, or server's partner in doubles, that it prevents the receiver from having a clear view of the ball. (The receiver is obligated to take up good court position, near center court, to obtain that view.)

IX. Serving before the Receiver is Ready. A serve is made while the receiver is not ready as described in Rule 3.5(II).

RULE 3.10 OUT SERVES

Any of the following results in an out:

I. Two Consecutive Fault Serves. See Rule 3.9.

II. Missed Serve Attempt. Any attempt to strike the ball that results in a total miss or in the ball touching any part of the server's body. Also, allowing the ball to bounce more than once during the service motion.

III. Touched Serve. Any served ball that on the rebound from the front wall touches the server or server's racquet before touching the floor, or any ball intentionally stopped or caught by the server or server's partner.

IV. Fake or Balk Serve. Any movement of the racquet toward the ball during the serve which is non-continuous and done for the purpose of deceiving the receiver. If a balk serve occurs, but the referee believes that no deceit was involved, the option of declaring "no serve" and having the serve replayed without penalty can be exercised.

V. Illegal Hit. An illegal hit includes contacting the ball twice, carrying the ball, or hitting the ball with the handle of the racquet or part of the body or uniform.

VI. Non-Front Wall Serve. Any served ball that does not strike the front wall first.

VII. Crotch Serve. Any served ball that hits the crotch of the front wall and floor, front wall and side wall, or front wall and ceiling is an out serve (because it did not hit the front wall first). A serve into the crotch of the back wall and floor is a good serve and in play. A served ball that hits the crotch of the side wall and floor beyond the short line is in play.

VIII. Out-of-Court Serve. An out-of-court serve is any served ball that first hits the front wall and, before striking the floor, either goes out of the court or hits a surface above the normal playing area of the court that has been declared as out-of-play for a valid reason [See Rule 2.1(I)].

IX. Safety Zone Violation. If the server, or doubles partner, enters into the safety zone before the served ball passes the short line, it shall result in the loss of serve.

RULE 3.11 RETURN OF SERVE

   I. Receiving Position
     A. The receiver may not enter the safety zone until the ball bounces or crosses the receiving line.
     B. On the fly return attempt, the receiver may not strike the ball until the ball breaks the plane of the receiving line. However, the receiver's follow-through may carry the receiver or the racquet past the receiving line.
     C. Neither the receiver nor the racquet may break the plane of the short line, except if the ball is struck after rebounding off the back wall.
     D. Any violation by the receiver results in a point for the server.
   II. Defective Serve. A player on the receiving side may not intentionally catch or touch a served ball (such as an apparently long or short serve) until the referee has made a call or the ball has touched the floor for a second time. Violation results in a point.
  III. Legal Return. After a legal serve, a player receiving the serve must strike the ball on the fly or after the first bounce, and before the ball touches the floor the second time; and return the ball to the front wall, either directly or after touching one or both side walls, the back wall or the ceiling, or any combination of those surfaces. A returned ball must touch the front wall before touching the floor.
  IV. Failure to Return. The failure to return a serve results in a point for the server.
   V. Other Provisions. Except as noted in this rule (3.11), the return of serve is subject to all provisions of Rules 3.13 through 3.15.

RULE 3.12 CHANGES OF SERVE

   I. Outs. A server is entitled to continue serving until one of the following occurs:
     A.   Out Serve. See Rule 3.10.
     B.   Two Consecutive Fault Serves. See Rule 3.9.
     C.   Failure to Return Ball. Player or team fails to keep the ball in play as required by Rule 3.11(III).
     D.   Avoidable Hinder. Player or team commits an avoidable hinder which results in an out. See Rule 3.15.
   II. Sideout. Retiring the server in singles is called a sideout.
  III. Effect of Sideout. When the server (or serving team) receives a sideout, the server becomes the receiver and the receiver becomes the server.

RULE 3.13 RALLIES

All of the play which occurs after the successful return of serve is called the rally. Play shall be conducted according to the following rules:

   I. Legal Hits. Only the head of the racquet may be used at any time to return the ball. The racquet may be held in one or both hands. Switching hands to hit a ball, touching the ball with any part of the body or uniform, or removing the wrist safety cord during a rally results in a loss of the rally.

II. One Touch. The player or team trying to return the ball may touch or strike the ball only once or else the rally is lost. The ball may not be carried. (A carried ball is one which rests on the racquet long enough that the effect is more of a sling or throw than a hit.)

III. Failure to Return. Any of the following constitutes a failure to make a legal return during a rally:
  A. The ball bounces on the floor more than once before being hit.
  B. The ball does not reach the front wall on the fly.
  C. The ball is hit such that it goes into the gallery or wall opening or else hits a surface above the normal playing area of the court that has been declared as out-of-play [See Rule 2.1(I)].
  D. A ball which obviously does not have the velocity or direction to hit the front wall strikes another player.
  E. A ball struck by one player on a team hits that player or that player's partner.
  F. Committing an avoidable hinder. See Rule 3.15.
  G. Switching hands during a rally.
  H. Failure to use a racquet wrist safety cord.
  I. Touching the ball with the body or uniform.
  J. Carrying or slinging the ball with the racquet.

IV. Effect of Failure to Return. Violations of Rules 3.13(I) through (III) result in a loss of rally. If the serving player or team loses the rally, it is an out. If the receiver loses the rally, it results in a point for the server.

V. Return Attempts. The ball remains in play until it touches the floor a second time, regardless of how many walls it makes contact with—including the front wall. If a player swings at the ball and misses it, the player may continue to attempt to return the ball until it touches the floor for the second time.

VI. Broken Ball. If there is any suspicion that a ball has broken during a rally, play shall continue until the end of the rally. The referee or any player may request the ball be examined. If the referee decides the ball is broken the ball will be replaced and the rally replayed. The server will get two serves. The only proper way to check for a broken ball is to squeeze it by hand. (Checking the ball by striking it with a racquet will not be considered a valid check and shall work to the disadvantage of the player or team which struck the ball after the rally.)

VII. Play Stoppage
  A. If a foreign object enters the court, or any other outside interference occurs, the referee shall stop the play immediately and declare a dead-ball hinder.
  B. If a player loses any apparel, equipment, or other article, the referee shall stop play immediately and declare an avoidable hinder or dead-ball hinder as described in Rule 3.15(IX).

VIII. Replays. Whenever a rally is replayed for any reason, the server is awarded two serves. A previous fault serve is not considered.

RULE 3.14 DEAD-BALL HINDERS

A rally is replayed without penalty and the server receives two serves whenever a dead-ball hinder occurs. Also, see Rule 3.15 which describes conditions under which a hinder might be declared avoidable and result in loss of the rally.

I. Situations
   A. Court Hinders. The referee should stop play immediately whenever the ball hits any part of the court that was designated in advance as a court hinder (such as a vent grate). The referee should also stop play (i) when the ball takes an irregular bounce as a result of contacting a rough surface (such as court light or vent) or after striking a wet spot on the floor or wall and (ii) when, in the referee's opinion, the irregular bounce affected the rally.
   B. Ball Hits Opponent. When an opponent is hit by a return shot in flight, it is a dead-ball hinder. If the opponent is struck by a ball which obviously did not have the velocity or direction to reach the front wall, it is not a hinder, and the player who hit the ball will lose the rally. A player who has been hit by the ball can stop play and make the call though the call must be made immediately and acknowledged by the referee. Note this interference may, under certain conditions, be declared an avoidable hinder. See Rule 3.15.
   C. Body Contact. If body contact occurs which the referee believes was sufficient to stop the rally, either for the purpose of preventing injury by further contact or because the contact prevented a player from being able to make a reasonable return, the referee shall call a hinder. Incidental body contact in which the offensive player clearly will have the advantage should not be called a hinder, unless the offensive player obviously stops play. Contact with the racquet on the follow-through normally is not considered a hinder.
   D. Screen Ball. Any ball rebounding from the front wall so close to the body of the defensive player that it prevents the offensive player from having a clear view of the ball. (The referee should be careful not to make the screen call so quickly that it takes away a good offensive opportunity.) A ball that passes between the legs of a player who has just returned the ball is not automatically a screen. It depends on whether the other player is impaired as a result. Generally, the call should work to the advantage of the offensive player.
   E. Backswing Hinder. Any body or racquet contact, on the backswing or on the way to or just prior to returning the ball, which impairs the hitter's ability to take a reasonable swing. This call can be made by the player attempting the return, though the call must be made immediately and is subject to the referee's approval. Note the interference may be considered an avoidable hinder. See Rule 3.15.
   F. Safety Holdup. Any player about to execute a return who believes that striking the opponent with the ball or racquet is likely, may immediately stop play and request a dead-ball hinder. This call must be made immediately and is subject to acceptance and approval of the referee. (The referee will grant a dead-ball hinder if it is believed the holdup was reasonable and the player would have been able to return the shot. The referee may also call an avoidable hinder if warranted.)
   G. Other Interference. Any other unintentional interference which prevents an opponent from having a fair chance to see or return the ball. Example: When a ball from another court enters the court during a rally or when a referee's call on an adjacent court obviously distracts a player.

II. Effect of Hinders. The referee's call of hinder stops play and voids any situation which follows, such as the ball hitting the player. The only hinders that may be called by a player are described in rules (B), (E), and (F) above, and all of these are subject to the approval of the referee. A dead-ball hinder stops play and the rally is replayed. The server receives two serves.

III. Responsibility. While making an attempt to return the ball, a player is entitled to a fair chance to see and return the ball. It is the responsibility of the side that has just hit the ball to move so the receiving side may go straight to the ball and have an unobstructed view of and swing at the ball. However, the receiver is responsible for making a reasonable effort to move towards the ball and must have a reasonable chance to return the ball for any type of hinder to be called.

RULE 3.15 AVOIDABLE HINDERS

An avoidable hinder results in the loss of the rally. An avoidable hinder does not necessarily have to be an intentional act. Dead-ball hinders are described in Rule 3.14. Any of the following results in an avoidable hinder:

I. Failure to Move. A player does not move sufficiently to allow an opponent a shot straight to the front wall as well as a cross-court shot which is a shot directly to the front wall at an angle that would cause the ball to rebound directly to the rear corner farthest from the player hitting the ball. Also when a player moves in such a direction that it prevents an opponent from taking either of these shots.

II. Stroke Interference. This occurs when a player moves, or fails to move, so that the opponent returning the ball does not have a free, unimpeded swing. This includes unintentionally moving in a direction which prevents the opponent from making an open, offensive shot.

III. Blocking. Moves into a position which blocks the opponent from getting to, or returning, the ball; or in doubles, a player moves in front of an opponent as the player's partner is returning the ball.

IV. Moving into the Ball. Moves in the way and is struck by the ball just played by the opponent.

V. Pushing. Deliberately pushes or shoves opponent during a rally.

VI. Intentional Distractions. Deliberate shouting, stamping of feet, waving of racquet, or any other manner of disrupting one's opponent.

VII. View Obstruction. A player moves across an opponent's line of vision just before the opponent strikes the ball.

VIII. Wetting the Ball. The players, particularly the server, should insure that the ball is dry prior to the serve. Any wet ball that is not corrected prior to the serve shall result in an avoidable hinder against the server.

IX. Apparel or Equipment Loss. If a player loses any apparel, equipment, or other article, play shall be immediately stopped and that player shall be called for an avoidable hinder, unless the player has just hit a shot that could not be retrieved. If the loss of equipment is caused by a player's opponent, then a dead-ball hinder should be called. If the opponent's action is judged to have been avoidable, then the opponent should be called for an avoidable hinder.

RULE 3.16 TIMEOUTS

I. Rest Periods. Each player or team is entitled to three 30-second timeouts in games to 15 and two 30-second timeouts in games to 11. Timeouts may not be called by either side after service motion has begun. Calling for a timeout when none remain or after service motion has begun, or taking more than 30 seconds in a timeout, will result in the assessment of a technical foul for delay of game.

II. Injury. If a player is injured during the course of a match as a result of contact, such as with the ball, racquet, wall or floor, an injury timeout will be awarded. While a player may call more than one timeout for the same injury or for additional injuries which occur during the match, a player is not allowed more than a total of 15 minutes of rest for injury during the entire match. If the injured player is not able to resume play after total rest of 15 minutes, the match shall be awarded to the opponent.

    A. Should any external bleeding occur, the referee must halt play as soon as the rally is over, charge an injury timeout to the person who is bleeding, and not allow the match to continue until the bleeding has stopped.

    B. Muscle cramps and pulls, fatigue, and other ailments that are not caused by direct contact on the court will not be considered an injury. Injury time is also not allowed for pre-existing conditions.

III. Equipment Timeouts. Players are expected to keep all clothing and equipment in good, playable condition and are expected to use regular timeouts and time between games for adjustment and replacement of equipment. If a player or team is out of timeouts and the referee determines that an equipment change or adjustment is necessary for fair and safe continuation of the match, the referee may grant an equipment timeout not to exceed 2 minutes. The referee may allow additional time under unusual circumstances.

IV. Between Games. The rest period between the first two games of a match is 2 minutes. If a tiebreaker is necessary, the rest period between the second and third game is 5 minutes.

V. Postponed Games. Any games postponed by referees shall be resumed with the same score as when postponed.

RULE 3.17 TECHNICAL FOULS AND WARNINGS

I. Technical Fouls. The referee is empowered to deduct one point from a player's or team's score when, in the referee's sole judgment, the player is being overtly and deliberately abusive. If the player or team against whom the technical foul was assessed does not resume play immediately, the referee is empowered to forfeit the match in favor of the opponent. Some examples of actions which can result in technical fouls are:

    A. Profanity.

    B. Excessive arguing.

    C. Threat of any nature to opponent or referee.

    D. Excessive or hard striking of the ball between rallies.

    E. Slamming of the racquet against walls or floor, slamming the door, or any action which might result in damage to the court or injury to other players.

    F. Delay of game. Examples include:

        1. Taking too much time to dry the court

        2. Excessive questioning of the referee about the rules

        3. Exceeding the time allotted for timeouts or between games

        4. Calling a timeout when none remain, or after the service motion begins

        5. Taking more than ten seconds to serve or be ready to receive serve.

G. Intentional front line foot fault to negate a bad lob serve.

H. Anything the referee considers to be unsportsmanlike behavior.

I. Failure to wear lensed eyewear designed for racquet sports [See Rule 2.5(I)] is an automatic technical foul on the first infraction, plus a mandatory timeout (to acquire the proper eyewear) will be charged against the offending player. A second infraction by that player during the match will result in automatic forfeiture of the match.

II. Technical Warnings. If a player's behavior is not so severe as to warrant a technical foul, a technical warning may be issued without the deduction of a point.

III. Effect of Technical Foul or Warning. If a referee issues a technical foul, one point shall be removed from the offender's score. No point will be deducted if a referee issues a technical warning. In either case, a technical foul or warning should be accompanied by a brief explanation. Issuing a technical foul or warning has no effect on who will be serving when play resumes. If a technical foul occurs when the offender has no points or between games, the result will be that the offender's score becomes minus one (-1).

RULE MODIFICATIONS

The following sections (4.0 through 11.0) detail the additional or modified rules that apply to variations of the singles game described in Sections 1 through 3.

DOUBLES

The USRA's rules for singles also apply in doubles with the following additions and modifications:

RULE 4.1 DOUBLES TEAM

I. A doubles team shall consist of two players who meet either the age requirements or player classification requirements to participate in a particular division of play. A team with different skill levels must play in the division of the player with the higher level of ability. When playing in an adult age division, the team must play in the division of the younger player. When playing in a junior age division, the team must play in the division of the older player.

II. A change in playing partners may be made so long as the first match of the posted team has not begun. For this purpose only, the match will be considered started once the teams have been called to the court. The team must notify the tournament director of the change prior to the beginning of the match.

RULE 4.2 SERVE IN DOUBLES

I. Order of Serve. Each team shall inform the referee of the order of service which shall be followed throughout that game. The order of serve may be changed between games. At the beginning of each game, when the first server of the first team to serve is out, the team is out. Thereafter, both players on each team shall serve until the team receives a handout and a sideout.

II. Partner's Position. On each serve, the server's partner shall stand erect with back to the side wall and with both feet on the floor within the service box from the moment the server begins the service motion until the served ball passes the short line. Violations are called foot faults. However, if the server's partner enters the safety zone before the ball passes the short line, the server loses service.

III. Changes of Serve. In doubles, the side is retired when both partners have lost service, except that the team which serves first at the beginning of each game loses the serve when the first server is retired.

RULE 4.3 FAULT SERVE IN DOUBLES

I. The server's partner is not in the service box with both feet on the floor and back to the side wall from the time the server begins the service motion until the ball passes the short line results in a fault serve.

II. A served ball that hits the doubles partner while in the doubles box results in a fault serve.

RULE 4.4 OUT SERVE IN DOUBLES

I. Out-of-Order Serve. In doubles, when either partner serves out of order, the points scored by that server will be subtracted and an out serve will be called: if the second server serves out of order, the out serve will be applied to the first server and the second server will resume serving. If the player designated as the first server serves out of order, a sideout will be called. The referee should call "no serve" as soon as an out-of-order serve occurs. If no points are scored while the team is out of order, only the out penalty will have to be assessed. However, if points are scored before the out of order condition is noticed and the referee cannot recall the number, the referee may enlist the aid of the line judges (but not the crowd) to recall the number of points to be deducted.

II. Ball Hits Partner. A served ball that hits the doubles partner while outside the doubles box results in loss of serve.

RULE 4.5 RETURN IN DOUBLES

I. The rally is lost if one player hits that same player's partner with an attempted return.

II.   If one player swings at the ball and misses it, both partners may make further attempts to return the ball until it touches the floor the second time. Both partners on a side are entitled to return the ball.

ONE SERVE

The USRA's standard rules governing racquetball play will be followed except for the following:

RULE 5.1 ONE SERVE

Only one serve is allowed. Therefore, any fault serve is an out serve, with a few exceptions.

RULE 5.2 SCREEN SERVE

If a serve is called a screen, the server will be allowed one more opportunity to hit a legal serve. Two consecutive screen serves results in an out.

RULE 5.3 SERVE HITS PARTNER

In doubles, if a serve hits the non-serving partner while standing in the box, the server will be allowed one more opportunity to hit a legal serve. Hitting the non-serving partner twice, results in an out.

RULE 5.4 CONSECUTIVE FAULTS

In doubles, either (i) a screen serve followed by hitting the non-serving partner or (ii) hitting the non-serving partner followed by a screen serve, results in an out.

MULTI-BOUNCE

In general, the USRA's standard rules governing racquetball play will be followed except for the modifications which follow.

RULE 6.1 BASIC RETURN RULE

In general, the ball remains in play as long as it is bouncing. However, the player may swing only once at the ball and the ball is considered dead at the point it stops bouncing and begins to roll. Also, anytime the ball rebounds off the back wall, it must be struck before it crosses the short line on the way to the front wall, except as explained in Rule 6.2.

RULE 6.2 BLAST RULE

If the ball caroms from the front wall to the back wall on the fly, the player may hit the ball from any place on the court—including past the short line—so long as the ball is still bouncing.

RULE 6.3 FRONT WALL LINES

Two parallel lines (tape may be used) should be placed across the front wall such that the bottom edge of one line is 3 feet above the floor and the bottom edge of the other line is 1 foot above the floor. During the rally, any ball that hits the front wall (i) below the 3-foot line and (ii) either on or above the 1-foot line must be returned before it bounces a third time. However, if the ball hits below the 1-foot line, it must be returned before it bounces twice. If the ball hits on or above the 3-foot line, the ball must be returned as described in the basic return rule.

RULE 6.4 GAMES AND MATCHES

All games are played to 11 points and the first side to win two games, wins the match.

ONE-WALL & THREE-WALL PLAY

In general, the USRA's standard rules governing racquetball play will be followed except for the modifications which follow.

RULE 7.1 ONE-WALL

There are two playing surfaces—the front wall and the floor. The wall is 20 feet wide and 16 feet high. The floor is 20 feet wide and 34 feet to the back edge of the long line. To permit movement by players, there should be a minimum of three feet (six feet is recommended) beyond the long line and six feet outside each side line.

   I. Short Line. The back edge of the short line is 16 feet from the wall.

  II. Service Markers. Lines at least six inches long which are parallel with, and midway between, the long and short lines. The extension of the service markers form the imaginary boundary of the service line.

 III. Service Zone. The entire floor area inside and including the short line, side lines and service line.

 IV. Receiving Zone. The entire floor area in back of the short line, including the side lines and the long line.

RULE 7.2 THREE-WALL WITH SHORT SIDE WALL

The front wall is 20 feet wide and 20 feet high. The side walls are 20 feet long and 20 feet high, with the side walls tapering to 12 feet high. The floor length and court markings are the same as a four wall court.

RULE 7.3 THREE-WALL WITH LONG SIDE WALL

The court is 20 feet wide, 20 feet high and 40 feet long. The side walls may taper from 20 feet high at the front wall down to 12 feet high at the end of the court. All court markings are the same as a four wall court.

RULE 7.4 SERVICE IN THREE-WALL COURTS

A serve that goes beyond the side walls on the fly is an out. A serve that goes beyond the long line on a fly, but within the side walls, is a fault.

WHEELCHAIR

RULE 8.1 CHANGES TO STANDARD RULES

In general, the USRA's standard rules governing racquetball play will be followed, except for the modifications which follow.

I.   Where USRA rules refer to server, person, body, or other similar variations, for wheelchair play such reference shall include all parts of the wheelchair in addition to the person sitting on it.

II. Where the rules refer to feet, standing or other similar descriptions, for wheelchair play it means only where the rear wheels actually touch the floor.

III. Where the rules mention body contact, for wheelchair play it shall mean any part of the wheelchair in addition to the player.

IV. Where the rules refer to double bounce or after the first bounce, it shall mean three bounces. All variations of the same phrases shall be revised accordingly.

RULE 8.2 DIVISIONS

I.   Novice Division. The novice division is for the beginning player who is just learning to play.

II. Intermediate Division. The Intermediate Division is for the player who has played tournaments before and has a skill level to be competitive in the division.

III. Open Division. The Open Division is the highest level of play and is for the advanced player.

IV. Multi-Bounce Division. The Multi-Bounce Division is for the individuals (men or women) whose mobility is such that wheelchair racquetball would be impossible if not for the Multi-Bounce Division.

V.   Junior Division. The junior divisions are for players who are under the age of 19. The tournament director will determine if the divisions will be played as two bounce or multi-bounce. Age divisions are: 8–11, 12–15, and 16–18.

RULE 8.3 RULES

I.   Two Bounce Rule. Two bounces are used in wheelchair racquetball in all divisions except the Multi-Bounce Division. The ball may hit the floor twice before being returned.

II. Out-of-Chair Rule. The player can neither intentionally jump out of the chair to hit a ball nor stand up in the chair to serve the ball. If the referee determines that the chair was left intentionally it will result in loss of the rally for the offender. If a player unintentionally leaves the chair, no penalty will be assessed. Repeat offenders will be warned by the referee.

III. Equipment Standards. To protect playing surfaces, the tournament officials will not allow a person to participate with black tires or anything which will mark or damage the court.

IV. Start. The serve may be started from any place within the service zone. Although the front casters may extend beyond the lines of the service zone, at no time shall the rear wheels cross either the service or short line before the served ball crosses the short line. Penalties for violation are the same as those for the standard game.

V. Maintenance Delay. A maintenance delay is a delay in the progress of a match due to a malfunction of a wheelchair, prosthesis, or assistive device. Such delay must be requested by the player, granted by the referee during the match, and shall not exceed 5 minutes. Only two such delays may be granted for each player for each match. After using both maintenance delays, the player has the following options:
A. Continue play with the defective equipment
B. Immediately substitute replacement equipment
C. Postpone the game, with the approval of the referee and opponent

RULE 8.4 MULTI-BOUNCE RULES

I. The ball may bounce as many times as the receiver wants though the player may swing only once to return the ball to the front wall.

II. The ball must be hit before it crosses the short line on its way back to the front wall.

III. The receiver cannot cross the short line after the ball contacts the back wall.

VISUALLY IMPAIRED

In general, the USRA's standard rules governing racquetball play will be followed except for the modifications which follow.

RULE 9.1 ELIGIBILITY

A player's visual acuity must not be better than 20/200 with the best practical eye correction or else the player's field of vision must not be better than 20 degrees. The three classifications of blindness are B1 (totally blind to light perception), B2 (able to see hand movement up to 20/600 corrected), and B3 (from 20/600 to 20/200 corrected).

RULE 9.2 RETURN OF SERVE AND RALLIES

On the return of a serve and on every return thereafter, the player may make multiple attempts to strike the ball until (i) the ball has been touched, (ii) the ball has stopped bouncing, or (iii) the ball has passed the short line after touching the back wall. The only exception is described in Rule 9.3.

RULE 9.3 BLAST RULE

If the ball (other than on the serve) caroms from the front wall to the back wall on the fly, the player may retrieve the ball from any place on the court—including in front of the short line— so long as the ball has not been touched and is still bouncing.

RULE 9.4 HINDERS

A dead-ball hinder will result in the rally being replayed without penalty unless the hinder was intentional. If a hinder is clearly intentional, an avoidable hinder should be called and the rally awarded to the non-offending player or team.

DEAF [NRAD]

In general, the USRA's standard rules governing racquetball play will be followed except for the modifications which follow.

RULE 10.1 ELIGIBILITY

An athlete shall have a hearing loss of 55 db or more in the better ear to be eligible for any NRAD tournament.

PROFESSIONAL [IRT/MEN & WIRT/WOMEN]

In general, competition on both the International Racquetball Tour [IRT] and Women's International Racquetball Tour [WIRT] will follow the standard rules governing racquetball established by the USRA, except for the modifications which follow. Modifications for both professional tours are consistent, with one exception as noted in Rule 11.4.

RULE 11.1 GAME, MATCH

All games are played to 11 points, and are won by the player who scores to that level, with a 2-point lead. If necessary, the game will continue beyond 11 points, until such time as one player has a 2-point lead. Matches are played the best three out of a possible five games to 11.

RULE 11.2 APPEALS

The referee's call is final. There are no line judges, and no appeals may be made.

RULE 11.3 SERVE

Players are allowed only one serve to put the ball into play.

RULE 11.4 SCREEN SERVE

In IRT matches, screen serves are replayed. In WIRT matches, two consecutive screen serves will result in a sideout.

RULE 11.5 COURT HINDERS

No court hinders are allowed or called.

RULE 11.6 OUT-OF-COURT BALL

Any ball leaving the court results in a loss of rally.

RULE 11.7 BALL

All matches are played with the Penn Pro ball. The first, third, and fifth (if necessary) games of the match are started with a new ball.

RULE 11.8 TIMEOUTS

I. Per Game. Each player is entitled to one 1-minute timeout per game.

II. Between Points. The player has 15 seconds from the end of the previous rally to put the ball in play.

III. Between Games. The rest period between all games is 2 minutes, including a fifth game tiebreaker.

IV. Equipment Timeouts. A player does not have to use regular timeouts to correct or adjust equipment, provided that the need for the change or adjustment is acknowledged by the referee as being necessary for fair and safe continuation of the match.

V. Injury Timeout. Consists of two $7\frac{1}{2}$ minute timeouts within a match. Once an injury timeout is taken, the full $7\frac{1}{2}$ minutes must be used, or it is forfeited.

COMPETITION POLICIES AND PROCEDURES

Sections A through D which follow contain mostly policies and procedures concerning competition, rather than "rules of play" which are subject to the formal rule change procedures. However, some of the topics that follow are still subject to the formal rule change procedures. In the next edition of the rulebook, they will be highlighted for ease of location.

TOURNAMENTS

A.1 DRAWS

I. If possible, all draws shall be made at least 2 days before the tournament commences. The seeding method of drawing shall be approved by the USRA.

II. At USRA National events, the draw and seeding committee shall be chaired by the USRA's Executive Director, National Tournament Director, and the host tournament director. No other persons shall participate in the draw or seeding unless at the invitation of the draw and seeding committee.

III. In local and regional tournaments the draw shall be the responsibility of the tournament director.

A.2 CONSOLATION MATCHES

I. Each entrant shall be entitled to participate in a minimum of two matches. Therefore, losers of their first match shall have the opportunity to compete in a consolation bracket of their own division. In draws of less than seven players, a round robin may be offered. See A.6 about how to determine the winner of a round robin event.

II. Consolation matches may be waived at the discretion of the tournament director, but this waiver must be in writing on the tournament application.

III. Preliminary consolation matches will be two of three games to 11 points. Semifinal and final matches will follow the regular scoring format.

A.3 SCHEDULING

I. Preliminary Matches. If one or more contestants are entered in both singles and doubles, they may be required to play both singles and doubles on the same day with little rest between matches. This is a risk assumed on entering two singles events or a singles and doubles event. If possible, the schedule should provide at least 1 hour of rest between matches.

II. Final Matches. Where one or more players has reached the finals in both singles and doubles, it is recommended that the doubles match be played on the day preceding the singles. This would assure more rest between the final matches. If both final matches must be played on the same day or night, the following procedure is recommended:
   A. The singles match be played first, and;
   B. A rest period of not less than 1 hour be allowed between the finals in singles and doubles.

A.4 NOTICE OF MATCHES

After the first round of matches, it is the responsibility of each player to check the posted schedules to determine the time and place of each subsequent match. If any change is made in the schedule after posting, it shall be the duty of the tournament director to notify the players of the change.

A.5 THIRD PLACE

Players are not required to play off for third place. However, for point standings, if one semifinalist wants to play off for third and the other semifinalist does not, the one willing to play shall be awarded third place. If neither semifinalist wishes to play off for 3rd then the points shall be totaled, divided by 2, and awarded evenly to both players.

A.6 ROUND ROBIN SCORING

The final positions of players or teams in round robin competition is determined by the following sequence:

I. Winner of the most matches;

II. In a two way tie, winner of the head-to-head match;

III. In a tie of three or more, the player who lost the fewest games is awarded the highest position.
   A. If a two way tie remains, the winner of the head-to-head match is awarded the higher position.
   B. If a multiple tie remains, the total "points scored against" each player in all matches will be tabulated and the player who had the least "points scored against" them is awarded the highest position. Note: Forfeits will count as a match won in two games. In cases where "points scored against" is the tiebreaker, the points scored by the forfeiting team will be discounted from consideration of "points scored against" all teams.

A.7 COURT ASSIGNMENTS

In all USRA sanctioned tournaments, the tournament director and/or USRA official in attendance may decide on a change of court after the completion of any tournament game, if such a change will accommodate better spectator conditions.

A.8 TOURNAMENT CONDUCT

In all USRA sanctioned tournaments, the referee is empowered to forfeit a match, if the conduct of a player or team is considered detrimental to the tournament and the game. See B.5(IV) and (V).

A.9 SPECTATOR CONDUCT

In the event of disruptive or threatening behavior on the part of any spectator, relative, parent, guardian or coach at any USRA sanctioned event, the tournament director or USRA official in attendance, either of their own accord or at the request of the referee, is empowered to enforce the following sanctions:

I. For the first offense: violator may watch, but not speak, while the athlete's match is being played.

II. For the second offense: violator may not watch the athlete's match, but may remain within the building.

III. For the third offense: violator will be removed from the club for the duration of the tournament, and pertinent authorities advised of the restriction. If a given situation so warrants, the tournament director or USRA official may invoke this sanction immediately and without previous offenses—in the interest of safety.

OFFICIATING

B.1 TOURNAMENT MANAGEMENT

All USRA sanctioned tournaments shall be managed by a tournament director, who shall designate the officials.

B.2 TOURNAMENT RULES COMMITTEE

The tournament director should appoint a tournament rules committee to resolve any disputes that the referee, tournament desk, or tournament director cannot resolve. The committee, composed of an odd number of persons, may include state or national officials, or other qualified individuals in attendance who are prepared to meet on short notice. The tournament director should not be a member of this committee.

B.3 REFEREE APPOINTMENT AND REMOVAL

The principal official for every match shall be the referee who has been designated by the tournament director, or a designated representative, and who has been agreed upon by all participants in the match. The referee's authority regarding a match begins once the players are called to the court. The referee may be removed from a match upon the agreement of all participants (teams in doubles) or at the discretion of the tournament director or the designated representative. In the event that a referee's removal is requested by one player or team and not agreed to by the other, the tournament director or the designated representative may accept or reject the request. It is suggested that the match be observed before determining what, if any, action is to be taken. In addition, two line judges and a scorekeeper may also be designated to assist the referee in officiating the match.

B.4 RULES BRIEFING

Before all tournaments, all officials and players shall be briefed on rules as well as local court hinders, regulations, and modifications the tournament director wishes to impose. The briefing should be reduced to writing. The current USRA rules will apply and be made available. Any modifications the tournament director wishes to impose must be stated on the entry form and be available to all players at registration.

B.5 REFEREES

I. Pre-Match Duties. Before each match begins, it shall be the duty of the referee to:
   A. Check on adequacy of preparation of court with respect to cleanliness, lighting and temperature.
   B. Check on availability and suitability of materials to include balls, towels, scorecards, pencils and timepiece necessary for the match.
   C. Check the readiness and qualifications of the line judges and scorekeeper. Review appeal procedures and instruct them of their duties, rules and local regulations.
   D. Go onto the court to make introductions; brief the players on court hinders (both designated and undesignated); identify any out-of-play areas (see rule 2.1(I); discuss local regulations and rule modifications for this tournament; and explain often misinterpreted rules.
   E. Inspect players' equipment; identify the line judges; verify selection of a primary and alternate ball.
   F. Toss coin and offer the winner the choice of serving or receiving.

II. Decisions. During the match, the referee shall make all decisions with regard to the rules. Where line judges are used, the referee shall announce all final judgments. If both players in singles and three out of four in a doubles match disagree with a call made by the referee, the referee is overruled, with the exception of technical fouls and forfeitures.

III. Protests. Any decision not involving the judgment of the referee will, on protest, be accorded due process as set forth in the constitution of the USRA. For the purposes of rendering a prompt decision regarding protests filed during the course of an ongoing tournament, the stages of due process will be: first to the tournament desk, then to the tournament director, and finally to the tournament rules committee. In those instances when time permits, the protest may be elevated to the state association or, when appropriate, to the national level as called for in the USRA constitution.

IV. Forfeitures. A match may be forfeited by the referee when:
   A. Any player refuses to abide by the referee's decision or engages in unsportsmanlike conduct.
   B. Any player or team who fails to report to play 10 minutes after the match has been scheduled to play. (The tournament director may permit a longer delay if circumstances warrant such a decision.)
   C. A game will be forfeited by the referee for using an illegal racquet as specified in Rule 2.4(V).

V. Defaults. A player or team may be forfeited by the tournament director or official for failure to comply with the tournament or host facility's rules while on the premises between matches, or for abuse of hospitality, locker room, or other rules and procedures.

VI. Spectators. The referee shall have jurisdiction over the spectators, as well as the players, while the match is in progress.

VII. Other Rulings. The referee may rule on all matters not covered in the USRA Official Rules. However, the referee's ruling is subject to protest as described in B.5(III).

B.6 LINE JUDGES

I. When Utilized. Two line judges should be used for semifinal and final matches, when requested by a player or team, or when the referee or tournament director so desires. However, the use of line judges is subject to availability and the discretion of the tournament director.

II. Replacing Line Judges. If any player objects to a person serving as a line judge before the match begins, all reasonable effort shall be made to find a replacement acceptable to the officials and players. If a player objects after the match begins, any replacement shall be at the discretion of the referee and/or tournament director.

III. Position of Line Judges. The players and referee shall designate the court location of the line judges. Any dispute shall be settled by the tournament director.

IV. Duties and Responsibilities. Line judges are designated to help decide appeals. In the event of an appeal, and after a very brief explanation of the appeal by the referee, the line judges must indicate their opinion of the referee's call.

V. Signals. Line judges should extend their arm and signal as follows:
A. Thumb up to show agreement with the referee's call
B. Thumb down to show disagreement
C. Hand open with palm facing down to indicate "no opinion" or that the play in question wasn't seen

VI. Manner of Response. Line judges should be careful not to signal until the referee announces the appeal and asks for a ruling. In responding to the referee's request, line judges should not look at each other, but indicate their opinions simultaneously in clear view of the players and referee. If at any time a line judge is unsure of which call is being appealed or what the referee's call was, the line judge should ask the referee to repeat the call and the appeal.

VII. Result of Response. The referee's call stands if at least one line judge agrees with the referee or if neither line judge has an opinion. If both line judges disagree with the referee, the referee must reverse the call. If one line judge disagrees with the referee and the other signals no opinion, the rally is replayed. Any replays, with the exception of appeals on the second serve itself, will result in two serves.

B.7 APPEALS

I. Appealable Calls and Non-Calls. In any match using line judges, a player may appeal any call or non-call by the referee, except for a technical foul or forfeiture.

II. How to Appeal. A verbal appeal by a player must be made directly to the referee immediately after the rally has ended. A player who believes there is an infraction to appeal, should bring it to the attention of the referee and line judges by raising the non-racquet hand at the time the perceived infraction occurs. The player is obligated to continue to play until the rally has ended or the referee stops play. The referee will recognize a player's appeal only if it is made before that player leaves the court for any reason including timeouts and game-ending rallies or, if that player doesn't leave the court, before the next serve begins.

III. Loss of Appeal. A player or team forfeits its right of appeal for that rally if the appeal is made directly to the line judges or, if the appeal is made after an excessive demonstration or complaint.

IV. Limit on Appeals. A player or team can make three appeals per game. However, if either line judge disagrees (thumb down) with the referee's call, that appeal will not count against the three-appeal limit. In addition, a potential game-ending rally may be appealed without charge against the limit—even if the three-appeal limit has been reached.

B.8 OUTCOME OF APPEALS

Everything except technical fouls and forfeitures can be appealed. The following outcomes cover several of the most common types of appeal, but not all possible appeals could be addressed. Therefore, referee's discretion and common sense should govern the outcomes of those appeals that are not covered herein:

I.   Skip Ball. If the referee makes a call of "skip ball," and the call is reversed, the referee then must decide if the shot in question could have been returned had play continued. If, in the opinion of the referee, the shot could have been returned, the rally shall be replayed. However, if the shot was not retrievable, the side which hit the shot in question is declared the winner of the rally. If the referee makes no call on a shot (thereby indicating that the shot did not skip), an appeal may be made that the shot skipped. If the "no call" is reversed, the side which hit the shot in question loses the rally.

II. Fault Serve. If the referee makes a call of fault serve and the call is reversed, the serve is replayed, unless if the referee considered the serve to be not retrievable, in which case a point is awarded to the server. If an appeal is made because the referee makes no call on a serve—thereby indicating that the serve was good—and the "no call" is reversed, it will result in second serve if the infraction occurred on the first serve or loss of serve if the infraction occurred on the second serve.

III. Out Serve. If the referee calls an "out serve," and the call is reversed, the serve will be replayed, unless the serve was obviously a fault too, in which case the call becomes fault serve. However, if the call is reversed and the serve was considered an ace, a point will be awarded. Also, if the referee makes no call on a serve—thereby indicating that the serve was good—but the "no call" is reversed, it results in an immediate loss of serve.

IV. Double Bounce Pickup. If the referee makes a call of two bounces, and the call is reversed, the rally is replayed, except if the player against whom the call was made hit a shot that could not have been retrieved, then that player wins the rally. (Before awarding a rally in this situation, the referee must be certain that the shot would not have been retrieved even if play had not been halted.) If an appeal is made because the referee makes no call thereby indicating that the get was not two bounces, and the "no call" is reversed, the player who made the two bounce pickup is declared the loser of the rally.

V. Receiving Line Violation (Encroachment). If the referee makes a call of encroachment, but the call is overturned, the serve shall be replayed unless the return was deemed irretrievable in which case a sideout (or possibly a handout in doubles) should be called. When an appeal is made because the referee made no call, and the appeal is successful, the server is awarded a point.

VI. Court Hinder. If the referee makes a call of court hinder during a rally or return of serve, the rally is replayed. If the referee makes no call and a player feels that a court hinder occurred, that player may appeal. If the appeal is successful, the rally will be replayed. A court hinder on a second serve results in only that serve being replayed.

B.9 RULE INTERPRETATIONS

If a player feels the referee has interpreted the rules incorrectly, the player may require the referee or tournament director to cite the applicable rule in the rulebook. Having discovered a misapplication or misinterpretation, the official must correct the error by replaying the rally, awarding the point, calling sideout, or taking other corrective measures.

ELIGIBILITY AND NATIONAL EVENTS

C.1 PROFESSIONAL

A professional is defined as any player who has accepted prize money regardless of the amount in any professional sanctioned (including IRT/WIRT) tournament or in any other tournament so deemed by the USRA Board of Directors. (Note: Any player concerned about the adverse effect of losing amateur status should contact the USRA National Office at the earliest opportunity to ensure a clear understanding of this rule and that no action is taken that could jeopardize that status.)

I. An amateur player may participate in a professional sanctioned tournament but will not be considered a professional (i) if no prize money is accepted or (ii) if the prize money received remains intact and placed in trust under USRA guidelines.

II. The acceptance of merchandise or travel expenses shall not be considered prize money, and thus does not jeopardize a player's amateur status.

C.2 RETURN TO AMATEUR STATUS

Any player who has been classified as a professional can re-establish amateur status by requesting, in writing, this desire to be reclassified as an amateur. This application shall be tendered to the Executive Director of the USRA or a designated representative, and shall become effective immediately as long as the player making application for reinstatement of amateur status has received no money in any tournament, as defined in C.1, for the past 12 months.

C.3 USRA ELIGIBILITY

I. Any current USRA member who has not been classified as a professional (See C.1) may compete in any USRA sanctioned tournament.

II. Any current USRA member who has been classified as a professional may compete in any event at a USRA sanctioned tournament that offers prize money or merchandise.

C.4 RECOGNIZED DIVISIONS

Title opportunities at national championships will be selected from the division lists which follow. Combined "Age + Skill" divisions may also be offered to provide additional competitive opportunities for non-open entrants. For ranking consistency, state organizations are encouraged to select from these recognized divisions when establishing competition in all sanctioned events.

I. Open Division. Any player with amateur status.

II. Open Adult Age Divisions. Eligibility is determined by the player's age on the first day of the tournament. Divisions are:
24 & under - Varsity
25+ - Junior Veterans
30+ - Veterans
35+ - Seniors
40+ - Veteran Seniors
45+ - Masters
50+ - Veteran Masters
55+ - Golden Masters
60+ - Veteran Golden Masters
65+ - Senior Golden Masters
70+ - Advanced Golden Masters
75+ - Super Golden Masters
80+ - Grand Masters
85+ - Super Grand Masters

III. Junior Age Divisions. Player eligibility is determined by the player's age on January 1st of the current calendar year. Divisions are:
18 & Under
16 & Under
14 & Under
12 & Under

10 & Under
8 & Under (regular rules)
8 & Under (multi-bounce rules)
6 & Under (regular rules)
6 & Under (multi-bounce rules)

IV. Skill Divisions. Player eligibility is determined by AmPRO skill level certification, or verification by a state association official, at the entered level.
A
B
C
D
Novice

V. Age + Skill Divisions. Player eligibility is determined by the player's age on the first day of the tournament, plus AmPRO skill level certification, or verification by a state association official, at the entered level. Such combinations may be offered as additional competition to players who do not fall into the "open" or designated skill levels of play. For example: 24–A/B · 30+ B · 35+ C/D · 40+ A · 65 + A/B, etc.

C.5 DIVISION COMPETITION BY GENDER

Men and women may compete only in events and divisions for their respective gender during regional and national tournaments. If there is not sufficient number of players to warrant play in a specific division, the tournament director may place the entrants in a comparably competitive division. Note: For the purpose of encouraging the development of women's racquetball, the governing bodies of numerous states permit women to play in men's divisions when a comparable skill level is not available in the women's divisions.

C.6 USRA REGIONAL CHAMPIONSHIPS

I. Adult Regional Tournaments
   A. Regional tournaments will be conducted at various metropolitan sites designated annually by the USRA and players may compete at any site they choose.
   B. A person may compete in any number of adult regional tournaments, but may not enter a championship division (as listed in C.4) after having won that division at a previous adult regional tournament that same year.
   C. A person cannot participate in more than two championship events at a regional tournament.
   D. Any awards or remuneration to a USRA National Championship will be posted on the entry blank.
   E. One-serve rules (see Rule 5.0) will be used in all open divisions at USRA National and Regional Championships. Their use is optional at other tournaments.

II. Junior Regional Tournaments. All provisions of C.6 (I) also apply to juniors, except:

A. Regional tournaments will be conducted within the following regions which are identified for the purposes of junior competition:
   1. Region 1—Maine, New Hampshire, Vermont, Massachusetts, Rhode Island, Connecticut
   2. Region 2—New York, New Jersey
   3. Region 3—Pennsylvania, Maryland, Virginia, Delaware, District of Columbia
   4. Region 4—Florida, Georgia
   5. Region 5—Alabama, Mississippi, Tennessee
   6. Region 6—Arkansas, Kansas, Missouri, Oklahoma
   7. Region 7—Texas, Louisiana
   8. Region 8—Wisconsin, Iowa, Illinois
   9. Region 9—West Virginia, Ohio, Michigan
   10. Region 10—Indiana, Kentucky
   11. Region 11—North Dakota, South Dakota, Minnesota, Nebraska
   12. Region 12—Arizona, New Mexico, Utah, Colorado
   13. Region 13—Montana, Wyoming
   14. Region 14—California, Hawaii, Nevada
   15. Region 15—Washington, Idaho, Oregon, Alaska
   16. Region 16—North Carolina, South Carolina
B. A junior may compete in any number of junior regional tournaments, but may not enter a division [as listed in C.4(III)] after having won that division at a previous junior regional tournament that same year.
C. The provisions of C.6(I)C may not apply if tournaments (singles/doubles or adults/juniors) are combined.

C.7 U.S. NATIONAL SINGLES AND DOUBLES CHAMPIONSHIPS

The U.S. National Singles and Doubles Tournaments are separate tournaments and are played on different dates. One serve rules (see Rule 5.0) will apply in all Open divisions.

I. Competition in an Adult Regional singles tournament is required to qualify for the National Singles Championship.
   A. Exception: Men of the age of 55 and over (55+), and women age 45 and over (45+), are not required to qualify for the National Singles Championship.
   B. Exception: Any player who competes in either a junior or intercollegiate regional preceding the National Singles, will not be required to compete in an Adult Regional event.
II. The National Tournament Director may handle the rating of each region and determine how many players shall qualify from each regional tournament.
III. If a region is oversubscribed, a playoff to qualify players in a division may be conducted the day prior to the start of a National Championship.

C.8 U.S. NATIONAL JUNIOR OLYMPIC CHAMPIONSHIPS

It will be conducted on a different date than all other National Championships and generally subject to the provisions of C.7.

C.9 U.S. NATIONAL HIGH SCHOOL CHAMPIONSHIPS

It will be conducted on a different date than all other National Championships.

C.10 U.S. NATIONAL INTERCOLLEGIATE CHAMPIONSHIPS

It will be conducted on a different date than all other National Championships.

C.11 U.S. OPEN RACQUETBALL CHAMPIONSHIPS

It will be conducted on a different date than all other National Championships, and include both pro and amateur competitive divisions.

PROCEDURES

D.1 RULE CHANGE PROCEDURES

To ensure the orderly growth of racquetball, the USRA has established specific procedures that are followed before a major change is made to the rules of the game.

NOTE: Changes to rules and regulations in Sections 1 through 10 must adhere to published rule change procedures. Remaining sections may be altered by vote of the USRA Board of Directors.*

I. Rule change proposals must be submitted in writing to the USRA National Office by June 1st. *NOTE: The Board of Directors has imposed a moratorium on rule changes that establishes the next deadline for submission of rule change* **proposals** *as June 1, 2001, which would set the earliest possible* **effective date** *as September 1, 2002. [See following timeline for procedural details.]*

II. The USRA Board of Directors will review all proposals at its October board meeting and determine which will be considered.

*The following "policies & procedures" segments are subject to stated rule change procedures outlined in D.1:

A.6 Round Robin Scoring
A.8 Tournament Conduct
B.5 (IV–VII) Forfeitures, Defaults ...
B.6 Line Judges
B.7 Appeals
B.8 Outcome of Appeals

III. Selected proposals will appear in RACQUETBALL Magazine—the official USRA publication—as soon as possible after the October meeting for comment by the general membership.

IV. After reviewing membership input and the recommendations of the National Rules Committee and National Rules Commissioner, the proposals are discussed and voted upon at the annual Board of Directors meeting in May.

V. Changes approved in May become effective on September 1st. Exception: changes in racquet specifications become effective two years later on September 1st.

VI. Proposed rules that are considered for adoption in one year, but are not approved by the Board of Directors in May of that year, will not be considered for adoption the following year.

D.2 USRA NATIONAL RULES COMMITTEE

Rich Clay, National Rules
Commissioner
3401 North Kedzie
Chicago, IL 60618
 773/539-1114 (Office)
 847/918-7407 (Home)

Michael Arnolt
Suite 307
3833 North Meridian Street
Indianapolis, IN 46208
 317/926-2766 (Office)
 317/259-1359 (Home)

Dan Davis
5304 Hollister Street
Houston, TX 77040
 817/666-9139 (Office)

Otto Dietrich
4244 Russet Court
Lilburn, GA 30047
 770/972-2303 (Home)

Jim Easterling
321 Village
Lansing, MI 48911
 517/887-0459 (Home)
 517/373-2399 (Office)

Lorraine Galloway
175-20 Wexford Terrace #7-5
Jamaica Estates, NY 11432
 718/739-4629 (Home)

Jim Gillhouse
2120 East Willamette Avenue
Colorado Springs, CO 80909
 719/471-0799 (Home)
 719/526-9636 (Office)

Mary Lyons
940 Penman Road
Neptune Beach, FL 32266
 904/270-2224 (Office)

Eric Muller
14002 Slater
Overland Park, KS 66221
 913/681-5219 (Home)

Annie Muniz
812 Woodstock
Bellaire, TX 77401
 713/659-3554 (Office)
 713/432-0881 (Home)

Carlton Vass
P.O. Box 31875
Charleston, SC 29417
 843/571-7889 (Office)
 843/574-9059 (Home)

RULEBOOK INDEX

COPYRIGHT NOTICE

The 1998–1999 USRA Official Rules of Racquetball are copyrighted. All rights reserved. These rules may not be reproduced, electronically scanned or downloaded, either in whole or in part, without written permission of the publisher. Copyright © 1998 USRA.

For information about reprint rights and fees, please contact: The United States Racquetball Association, 1685 West Uintah, Colorado Springs, CO 80904-2921.
Tel: 719/635-5396
Fax: 719/635-0685
E-mail: rbzine@webaccess.net
http://www.usra.org.

REFERENCE MATERIALS

SUGGESTED READING

Fabian, L. & Hiser, J. (1986) *Racquetball: Strategies for Winning*. Dubuque, Iowa: Eddie B.

Stafford, R. (1990) *Racquetball: The Sport for Everyone* (3rd ed.). Memphis: Stafford.

Adams, L. & Goldbloom E. (1991) *Racquetball Today*. St. Paul, Minn.: West Publishing.

OTHER READING

Advanced Racquetball	S. Strandemo
Beginner Racquetball	J. Kramer
Contemporary Racquetball	C. Sheftel
Efficiency Racquet Sports	Hagerman
Enjoying Racquet Sports	The Diagram Group
How to Win at Racquetball	V. Spear
Inside Racquetball	C. Leve
Playing the Racquets	Morgenstern
Racquetball	Alison & Witbeck
Racquetball	B. Verner
Racquetball Basic Skills & Drills	B. Verner
Racquetball for Everyone	Isaacs, Lumplin & Schroer
Racquetball for the Serious Player	C. Garfinkel
Racquetball for Winners	M. Ishguro (Japanese)
Racquetball for Women	J. Sauser
Racquetball Made Easy	Lubarsky, Delson & Scagnetti
Racquetball Primer	Henkin

Racquetball Rules & Techniques Illustrated	G. Sullivan
Racquetball Step by Step	M. Mjehovich
Racquetball (Sports for Leisure Series)	Pangrazi
Racquetball: The Cult	Scott
Retailing in a Racquetball Pro Shop	Ektelon
Roll Out Racquetball	C. Brumfield
Teaching Your Child Racquetball	J. Sauser w/A. Shay
The Complete Book of Racquetball	S. Strandemo
The Racquetball Book	S. Strandemo
The Technique of Winning Racquetball	L. Pretner
Winning Racquetball	A. Shay w/C. Leve

INDEX